Great Escapes
South America

Photos by Tuca Reinés   *Edited by* Angelika Taschen   *Texts by* Christiane Reiter

Great Escapes
South America

TASCHEN

HONG KONG KÖLN LONDON LOS ANGELES MADRID PARIS TOKYO

Nothing is certain, but all things are possible.
Peruvian saying

If you look after your land, the trees and all of nature will shed their light.
It is then that we know we can benefit greatly from the earth.
Inca saying

He who has once drunk the waters of the Amazon will always return.
Brazilian saying

● 348 Hotel San Pedro de Majagua

● 340 Kapawi Ecolodge & Reserve

● 008 Pousada Maravilha

● 332 Hotel Monasterio

● 018 Txai Resort
● 028 Hotel Toca do Marlin
Vila Naiá – Paralelo 17° 078 ● 036 Hotel da Praça
Fazenda São Francisco do Corumbau 088 ● 048 Estrela d'Água
● 322 Hotel de Sal
058 Pousada Etnia
068 Ponta do Camarão

explora en Atacama 310 ●

● 110 Yacutinga Lodge
124 Posada La Bonita

Bodega El Esteco de Cafayate 132 ●

Hotel Casa Real 294 ●
● 140 Pirá Lodge

Dos Lunas 148
Estancia La Paz 160 ●
● 094 La Posada del Faro
102 La Posada Estancia Agua Verde
● 168 Estancia Ancón
174 Los Alamos
● 182 La Becasina Delta Lodge
190 La Escondida
Hotel del Casco 230 ●
200 Estancia El Rosario de Areco
Hotel Antumalal 274 ●
206 Estancia La Candelaria
216 Estancia Santa Rita

● 240 Ten Rivers Lodge
● 244 Estancia Arroyo Verde

explora en Patagonia 264 ●

● 254 Los Notros

Contents Inhalt Sommaire

Price categories:
$	up to 150 US$
$$	up to 250 US$
$$$	up to 450 US$
$$$$	over 450 US$

Preiskategorien:
$	bis 150 US$
$$	bis 250 US$
$$$	bis 450 US$
$$$$	über 450 US$

Catégories de prix:
$	jusqu'à 150 US$
$$	jusqu'à 250 US$
$$$	jusqu'à 450 US$
$$$$	plus de 450 US$

The play of light...
Pousada Maravilha, Fernando de Noronha

Pousada Maravilha, Fernando de Noronha

The play of light

When Portuguese merchant Fernando de Noronha discovered the 21-island archipelago off the north-eastern coast of Brazil in 1503, he took little interest in it – after a cursory inspection of the bizarre formations of volcanic rock, he took to the ocean again, looking for greater adventures. Others who followed him stayed longer, though not always of their own free will – in the 18th century the main island was made a penal colony, and around 1930 a gaol for political prisoners was established. In the Second World War it was an air base, and in the Sixties a NASA satellite observation post. Tourism did not take off till Fernando de Noronha was declared a nature reserve in 1988. Since then, it has earned a name as one of Brazil's best diving areas, celebrated for its dolphins and turtles in particular. Those who aren't so interested in the underwater world, but are happy to enjoy a unique experience on dry land, will relish a stay at the Pousada Maravilha. The eight bungalows blend in naturally with their setting by a magical bay – the wood replicates the hues of the rocks, the pool picks up the blue of the sky and the ocean. Relax on cream futons or gently swaying hammocks. The occasional strong notes of colour – cushions or crockery – are the only added extras the design permits itself; otherwise, a purist tone is dominant, showing in the most appealing of ways just how well the simple life and luxury can go together.

Book to pack: "The Lizard's Smile" by João Ubaldo Ribeiro

Pousada Maravilha
BR 363, s/n° – Sueste
Fernando de Noronha
Brazil
CEP 053990000
Tel. (55) 8136190028 and -1290
Fax (55) 8136190162
E-mail: reservas@pousadamaravilha.com.br
Website: www.pousadamaravilha.com.br
www.great-escapes-hotels.com

DIRECTIONS	350 km/225 miles off the north-east coast of Brazil, with daily flights from Natal and Recife
RATES	$$$$
ROOMS	5 bungalows for 2 people, 3 apartments for 4 people max.
FOOD	A delightful restaurant serving Mediterranean specialities. Room service is available
HISTORY	The first luxury hideaway on Fernando de Noronha
X-FACTOR	Purist design hotel affording plenty of privacy

Lichterspiele

Als der portugiesische Kaufmann Fernando de Noronha das
Archipel mit 21 Inseln vor der Nordostküste Brasiliens 1503
entdeckte, interessierte es ihn kaum – nach wenigen Blicken
auf das bizarr geformte Vulkangestein stach er wieder in See
und segelte vermeintlich größeren Abenteuern entgegen.
Andere, die nach ihm kamen, hielten es länger aus – wenn
auch nicht immer ganz freiwillig: Im 18. Jahrhundert wurde
die Hauptinsel zur Strafkolonie, um 1930 richtete man hier
ein politisches Gefängnis ein. Im Zweiten Weltkrieg diente
sie als Luftwaffenstützpunkt und in den sechziger Jahren
als Satellitenbeobachtungsposten der NASA. Der Tourismus
begann erst, als Fernando de Noronha 1988 zum Natur-
schutzgebiet erklärt wurde – seitdem gilt es als eines der
besten Tauchreviere Brasiliens und ist vor allem für seine
Delfine und Meeresschildkröten berühmt. Wer sich nicht
nur für die Unterwasserwelt interessiert, sondern auch an
Land Einzigartiges erleben möchte, zieht am besten in die
Pousada Maravilha. An einer zauberhaften Bucht passen
sich die acht Bungalows wie selbstverständlich ihrer Umgebung an – das Holz nimmt den Farbton der Felsen auf, der
Pool scheint direkt ins Blau von Himmel und Meer zu flie-
ßen, man entspannt auf cremefarbenen Futons oder in sanft
schwingenden Hängematten. Ein paar Farbtupfer – Kissen
oder Geschirr – sind die einzigen Extras, die sich das Design
gönnt; ansonsten dominiert hier der Purismus und zeigt auf
angenehmste Weise, wie gut *simple life* und Luxus zusam-
menpassen können.
Buchtipp: »Das Lächeln der Eidechse« von João Ubaldo Ribeiro

Jeux de lumière

Lorsque le marchand portugais Fernando de Noronha a
découvert en 1503 cet archipel qui fait face à la côte nord-est
du Brésil, on ne peut pas dire que les 21 îles l'aient captivé.
Après avoir jeté quelques coups d'œil sur les roches volca-
niques aux formes bizarres, il leva l'ancre et s'en alla vers
de nouvelles aventures. D'autres sont venus après lui, mais
ceux-là sont restés plus longtemps, et pas toujours de leur
plein gré : au 18e siècle, en effet, l'île principale devint un
pénitencier, en 1930 on y construisit une prison politique.
Au cours de la Deuxième Guerre mondiale, elle a servi de
base aérienne et dans les années 60, la N.A.S.A. y a installé
un poste d'observation de satellites. Et puis Fernando de
Norhona a été déclaré site naturel protégé, et le tourisme
a fait son apparition. Aujourd'hui, l'endroit est considéré
comme l'une des meilleures zones de plongée du Brésil et
il est renommé pour ses dauphins et ses tortues de mer.
La Pousada Maravilha est faite pour ceux qui non seulement
s'intéressent au monde sous-marin mais aussi aux richesses
uniques de la terre ferme. Les huit bungalows s'harmonisent
tout naturellement avec le paysage de la baie superbe qui les
entoure – le bois prend la couleur des rochers, la piscine
semble couler dans le bleu du ciel et de la mer ; les futons
couleur crème et les hamacs qui oscillent doucement sont
propices à la détente. Les quelques accents de couleur des
coussins et de la vaisselle sont les seuls « manquements »
au design délibérément puriste qui montre avec beaucoup
de charme combien la simplicité et le luxe font bon ménage.
Livre à emporter : « Le sourire du lézard »
de João Ubaldo Ribeiro

ANREISE	350 Kilometer vor Brasiliens Nordostküste gelegen, tägliche Flüge ab Natal und Recife
PREISE	$$$$
ZIMMER	5 Bungalows für 2 Personen, 3 Apartments für maximal 4 Personen
KÜCHE	Schönes Restaurant mit mediterranen Spezialitäten, Zimmerservice möglich
GESCHICHTE	Das erste Luxus-Hideaway auf Fernando de Noronha
X-FAKTOR	Puristisches Designhotel mit viel Privatsphäre

ACCÈS	Situé à 350 kilomètres de la côte nord-est du Brésil, vols journaliers à partir de Natal et Recife
PRIX	$$$$
CHAMBRES	5 bungalows pour 2 personnes, 3 appartements pour 4 personnes maximum
RESTAURATION	Le beau restaurant offre des spécialités méditerra-néennes, service de chambre possible
HISTOIRE	Le premier « refuge » de luxe sur Fernando de Noronha
LE « PETIT PLUS »	Le goût de la simplicité et beaucoup d'intimité

In the Garden of Eden...
Txai Resort, Bahia

Txai Resort, Bahia

In the Garden of Eden

Itacaré is in the south of Bahia, on the Cocoa Coast. In the mid-19th century, the "black gold" made it famous, and it became the foremost port of export in the region. Brazil's great writer Jorge Amado immortalised that cocoa boom in his novel "Gabriela, Clove and Cinnamon" – Amado was born in the region himself, on a cocoa plantation near Ilhéus. But ever since 1989 a fungal blight has annually been wiping out almost the entire crop all along the entire coast, and with it the regional economy – which has made tourism all the more important. One of the most appealing destinations is the Txai Resort, set amid a 100-hectare coconut grove which looks like a soft green pillow from the air. In the language of the Kaxinawa Indians, "Txai" means "companion", and in the spirit of this philosophy every guest is received as a family friend. The bungalows, built up on stilts, have all the distinctive atmosphere of private homes, and are furnished in the snug, rustic style of Bahia – no superfluous frills, dark wood, light fabrics, and colour-washed walls. The moment you wake you're looking at a picture-book natural setting, through the gossamer haze of the mosquito net. You can idle the day away on a recliner or at the beach, and succumb to the rhythms of Brazilian music in the evening. The resort supports re-afforestation projects and offers natural history excursions into the surrounding area. There's also a spa for relaxing massages, and yoga classes, and a restaurant where you can feed your eyes on the fabulous view as you dine on phenomenal fish.

Book to pack: "Gabriela, Clove and Cinnamon" by Jorge Amado

Txai Resort	
Rodovia Ilhéus Itacaré km 48	
Itacaré	
Bahia, Brazil	
CEP 45530 000	
Tel. and Fax (55) 7321015000	
E-mail: reserva@txairesort.com.br	
Website: www.txai.com.br	
www.great-escapes-hotels.com	

DIRECTIONS	15 km/10 miles south of Itacaré, 50 minutes by road from Ilhéus airport (transfer can be arranged on request)
RATES	$$$$
ROOMS	16 bungalows, 10 suites (for 2)
FOOD	Restaurant serving Bahian dishes such as "moqueca" (seafood and fish)
HISTORY	Opened eight years ago
X-FACTOR	It's like spending your vacation with good friends

Im Garten Eden

Itacaré liegt im Süden von Bahia, direkt an der Kakaoküste –
und wurde dank des »schwarzen Goldes« Mitte des 19. Jahr-
hunderts berühmt und zum größten Exporthafen der Region.
Dem Kakao-Boom setzte sogar Brasiliens großer Dichter
Jorge Amado mit seinem Roman »Gabriela wie Zimt und
Nelken« ein Denkmal – Amado stammt selbst aus der Ge-
gend, er wurde auf einer Kakaoplantage in der Nähe von
Ilhéus geboren. Seit 1989 jedoch zerstört ein Pilz Jahr für
Jahr fast die gesamte Ernte entlang der Küste und drückt die
Wirtschaft zu Boden – umso wichtiger wird der Tourismus.
Eine der sympathischsten Adressen ist das Txai Resort in-
mitten eines 100 Hektar großen Kokoshains, der aus der
Vogelperspektive wie ein weiches grünes Kissen aussieht.
In der Sprache der Kaxinawa-Indianer bedeutet »Txai« soviel
wie »Gefährte«, und dieser Philosophie zufolge wird hier
jeder Gast wie ein Freund der Familie empfangen. Die auf
Stelzen gebauten Bungalows besitzen das Flair eines Privat-
hauses, sind im rustikal-gemütlichen Stil Bahias eingerichtet – ohne viel Schnickschnack, mit dunklem Holz, hellen
Stoffen und bunt getünchten Wänden. Schon beim Auf-
wachen blickt man in eine Bilderbuchnatur, vor der das
Moskitonetz wie ein zarter Nebel hängt, lässt den Tag auf
der Sonnenliege oder am Strand verstreichen und sich
abends vom Rhythmus brasilianischer Musik einfangen.
Zudem unterstützt das Resort Aufforstungsprojekte und bietet naturkundliche Ausflüge in die Umgebung an, besitzt
ein Spa für entspannende Massagen und Yogastunden sowie
ein Restaurant, in dem man nicht nur fantastischen Fisch,
sondern auch einen fantastischen Ausblick genießt.

Buchtipp: »Gabriela wie Zimt und Nelken« von Jorge Amado

Au jardin d'Éden

Itacaré est située au sud de Bahia, sur la Côte du cacao.
Celui-ci a fait sa fortune au milieu du 19e siècle et l'a transformée en plus grand port d'exportation de la région. Le
grand écrivain brésilien Jorge Amado, lui-même né dans
une plantation à proximité d'Ilhéus, a d'ailleurs dressé un
monument au cacao avec son roman «Gabriela, girofle et
cannelle». Cependant, depuis 1989, une maladie dite «balai
de la sorcière» détruit les plantations. Sur le plan économique, le tourisme acquiert donc une importance capitale.
Le Txai Resort est l'une des adresses les plus sympathiques.
Il est situé au milieu d'une plantation de cacao de 100 hectares – vue du ciel, elle ressemble à un grand coussin vert.
Dans la langue des Indiens Kaxinava, «Txai» signifie «com-
pagnon», et chaque hôte est vraiment reçu comme un ami
de la famille. Les bungalows sur pilotis ont l'atmosphère de
maisons particulières, elles sont aménagées dans le style
bahianais tout de simplicité rustique et de confort, avec
des bois sombres, des étoffes claires et des murs aux vives
couleurs. Dès que l'on ouvre les yeux le matin, on distingue
une végétation enchanteresse derrière le fin voilage de la
moustiquaire ; on passe la journée sur une chaise longue ou
à la plage et la soirée à écouter, captivé, des rythmes brési-
liens. L'hôtel soutient des projets de reboisement et propose
des expéditions d'étude aux alentours. Il possède aussi un
centre de remise en forme qui offre des massages et des
cours de yoga, ainsi qu'un restaurant dans lequel on peut
déguster un poisson exquis en jouissant d'une vue fantastique.

**Livre à emporter : «Gabriela, girofle et cannelle»
de Jorge Amado**

ANREISE	15 Kilometer südlich von Itacaré gelegen, 50 Fahrtminu-ten vom Flughafen Ilhéus entfernt (Transfer auf Wunsch)
PREISE	$$$$
ZIMMER	16 Bungalows, 10 Suiten (für je 2 Personen)
KÜCHE	Restaurant mit bahianischen Gerichten wie »moqueca« (Meeresfrüchte & Fisch)
GESCHICHTE	Vor acht Jahren eröffnet
X-FAKTOR	Ferien wie bei guten Freunden

ACCÈS	Situé à 15 kilomètres au sud d'Itacaré, à 50 minutes de l'aéroport Ilhéus (transfert sur demande)
PRIX	$$$$
CHAMBRE	16 bungalows, 10 suites (pour 2 personnes)
RESTAURATION	Le restaurant propose des spécialités bahianaises comme la «moqueca» (fruits de mer et poisson)
HISTOIRE	Ouvert il y a huit ans
LE « PETIT PLUS »	Passer les vacances chez des amis

In search of new horizons...

Hotel Toca do Marlin, Bahia

In search of new horizons

The villas and country residences built in the finest locations in South America and on the east coast of the United States have long since established Bennett Nisencwajg as the architect of choice for high society. For the Hotel Toca do Marlin, he selected a dream setting: a coconut plantation on one of Bahia's most beautiful beaches, with two and a half kilometres (one and a half miles) of sand between the grounds and the cobalt-blue Atlantic. Toca do Marlin claims to be the first 6-star hotel on Bahia's south coast, and is lavish with superlatives in the eleven suites. Antiques are tellingly placed in spacious rooms furnished with teak and mahogany, with Spanish tiles and Italian marble. Dry off with towels of Egyptian cotton, eat from French porcelain, and lay your head on down pillows from Switzerland. A vacation here is sheer luxury – and, while it's quiet, it's never remotely dull. For the hotel is part of the do Cavalo Marinho resort, which is also home to the Haras Vale da Raposa stud farm, serving accoladed dressage horses from South America and Europe. If exploring the coast on horseback isn't your thing, cast off for some deep-sea fishing and go after the great fish after which the hotel is named. The waters of Bahia are home to the imperial blue marlin, the king of the seas, which grows up to four metres or thirteen feet in length and can weigh 700 kilograms (over 1,500 pounds). Fishing is a true adventure here, though one with a high price tag: an outing of eight to ten hours, for up to four persons costs around US$ 1,500.

Book to pack: "Where were you at night?" by Clarice Lispector

Hotel Toca do Marlin Estrada BA-001 km 40,5 Povoado de Santo André Santa Cruz Cabrália Bahia, Brazil Tel. (55) 7336715041 Fax (55) 7336715011 E-mail: tocadomarlin@tocadomarlin.com.br Website: www.tocadomarlin.com.br www.great-escapes-hotels.com	

DIRECTIONS	Situated 30 km/19 miles north of Porto Seguro international airport (near Santo André). Transfer is organised, by helicopter or road and boat
RATES	$$
ROOMS	2 Junior Suites, 8 Master Suites, 1 Presidential Suite
FOOD	The finest international cuisine, with a French touch
HISTORY	Opened in December 2000 as "the first 6-star hotel" in southern Bahia
X-FACTOR	A big one!

Zu neuen Horizonten

Als Privatarchitekt der Highsociety ist Bennett Nisencwajg
längst kein unbeschriebenes Blatt mehr – seine Villen und
Landsitze stehen an den schönsten Orten Südamerikas und
an der Ostküste der Vereinigten Staaten. Auch für das Hotel
Toca do Marlin hat er sich eine Traumkulisse ausgesucht:
eine Kokosplantage an einem der schönsten Strände von
Bahia – zweieinhalb Kilometer Sand liegen zwischen dem
Gelände und dem kobaltblauen Atlantik. Toca do Marlin
nimmt für sich in Anspruch, das erste 6-Sterne-Hotel an
Bahias Südküste zu sein, und geizt in den elf Suiten nicht
mit Superlativen. In den weiten Räumen sind Antiquitäten
wirkungsvoll in Szene gesetzt; man residiert inmitten von
Teakholz und Mahagoni, bestaunt spanische Kacheln und
italienischen Marmor, trocknet sich mit Handtüchern aus
ägyptischer Baumwolle ab, isst von französischem Porzellan
und schläft auf Daunenkissen aus der Schweiz. Es ist ein
luxuriös ruhiger Urlaub, den man hier verbringt – der aber
von Langweile meilenweit entfernt ist. Denn das Hotel ist
Teil des Resorts do Cavalo Marinho, das auch das berühmte
Gestüt »Haras Vale da Raposa« besitzt und dort preisgekrön-
te Dressurpferde aus Südamerika und Europa versorgt. Wer
die Küste nicht hoch zu Ross erkunden möchte, kann auch
zum Hochseefischen ablegen und auf die Jagd nach dem
Namensgeber des Hotels gehen. In den Gewässern vor
Bahia ist der Imperial Blue Marlin zu Hause, der König
der Meere, der bis zu vier Meter lang und 700 Kilogramm
schwer werden kann. Angler erwartet hier ein echtes Abenteuer, das allerdings seinen Preis hat: Der acht- bis zehn-
stündige Ausflug für maximal vier Personen kostet ungefähr
1.500 Dollar.

Buchtipp: »Wo warst Du in der Nacht?« von Clarice Lispector

Vers de nouveaux horizons

Concepteur de résidences exclusives, l'architecte et entrepreneur brésilien Bennett Nisencwajg n'est pas un inconnu –
ses constructions s'élèvent sur les plus beaux sites d'Amérique latine et sur la côte est des États-Unis. Son Hotel Toca
do Marlin ne fait pas exception, planté dans un décor de
rêve, au milieu de plantations cocotières sur l'une des plus
belles plages de Bahia – deux kilomètres de sable fin le
séparent des vagues couleur d'encre de l'Atlantique.
Toca do Marlin se targue d'être le premier hôtel six étoiles
sur la côte sud de Bahia, et ses onze suites dépassent toutes
les espérances. Des antiquités sont agréablement mises en
scène dans les vastes espaces ; l'hôte est entouré de teck et
d'acajou, de dalles espagnoles et de marbres italiens ; il s'es-
suie les mains sur les plus fins cotons égyptiens ; il mange
dans des assiettes de porcelaine française et dort sous des
édredons de duvet suisses.
Le cadre est luxueux et paisible – mais les activités sont
aussi au rendez-vous. Il faut dire que l'hôtel fait partie du
Resort do Cavalo Marinho qui possède aussi les célèbres
haras « Vale da Raposa », spécialistes de l'élevage et du dressage de Lusitans. Quant à l'amateur de sensations fortes,
il peut aussi partir en haute mer pêcher le poisson qui a
donné son nom à l'hôtel.
En effet, le prince des marlins, le Marlin Bleu Impérial qui
peut atteindre 4 mètres de long et peser 700 kilos, est chez
lui dans ces eaux chaudes. Le pêcher est une aventure qui
a son prix : l'excursion de huit à dix heures pour quatre personnes maximum coûte à peu près 1.500 dollars.

**Livre à emporter : « Où étais-tu pendant la nuit ? »
de Clarice Lispector**

ANREISE	30 Kilometer nördlich des Internationalen Flughafens Porto Seguro gelegen (bei Santo André). Der Transfer per Helikopter oder Auto und Boot wird organisiert
PREISE	$$
ZIMMER	2 Junior Suiten, 8 Master Suiten, 1 Presidential Suite
KÜCHE	Feinste internationale Menüs mit französischem Touch
GESCHICHTE	Im Dezember 2000 als »erstes 6-Sterne-Hotel« im Süden Bahias eröffnet
X-FAKTOR	Ein ausgezeichneter Fang!

ACCÈS	Situé à 30 kilomètres au nord de l'aéroport internatio- nal de Porto Seguro (près de Santo André). Transfert organisé par hélicoptère ou par voiture et bateau
PRIX	$$
CHAMBRES	2 Junior Suites, 8 Master Suites, 1 Presidential Suite
RESTAURATION	Cuisine internationale raffinée aux accents français
HISTOIRE	Premier hôtel « six étoiles » ouvert au sud de Bahia en décembre 2000
LE « PETIT PLUS »	Galopades et pêche au gros !

A hideaway in the greenery...

Hotel da Praça, Bahia

Hotel da Praça, Bahia

A hideaway in the greenery

There is surely no better address in Trancoso: Hotel da Praça is situated on the Quadrado, the main square of this former Jesuit settlement – also known in the past by the name of Pousada do Quadrado. In September 2006 the architects Bia Bittencourt and Ricardo Salem totally redesigned the hotel, paying homage to the art and culture of Trancoso. Almost all the furniture and accessories are by local craftspeople and designers. The airy rooms are decorated with solid woods and natural fibres, cheerfully striped fabrics and colourfully painted tiles. Not one of the eleven rooms resembles the other – and for those who want to spend a totally private holiday here, the simple but charming beach-house can be rented directly on the sandy beach. The guests are also close to nature in the gardens of the Hotel da Praça, which seem like an enchanted jungle thanks to centuries-old trees and exotic plants. There is a small surprise awaiting guests at the Japaiano restaurant: traditional Bahia dishes are combined with Japanese specialities to produce a refined fusion cuisine – and creations such as Sushi de Moqueca taste unusual but excellent. After a culinary trip around the world you return to Trancoso pure again in the bar, where the evening can be completed with Bahia drinks and music.

Book to pack: "Dona Flor and her Two Husbands" by Jorge Amado

Hotel da Praça	
Trancoso	
Bahia	
Brazil	
Tel. (55) 7336682121	
E-mail: reservas@hoteldapraca.com.br	
Website: www.hoteldapraca.com.br	
www.great-escapes-hotels.com	

DIRECTIONS	Situated 40 km/25 miles south of Porto Seguro international airport. Transfer by road, or by ferry (Porto Seguro-Arraial d'Ajuda) and road
RATES	$$
ROOMS	8 apartments, 2 suites, 1 beach-house
FOOD	Japanese cuisine with a Brazilian touch in the Restaurant Japaiano
HISTORY	The former Pousada do Quadrado was transformed into the Hotel da Praça in 2006
X-FACTOR	Living in the new old style of Bahia

Ein Versteck im Grünen

Eine bessere Adresse kann man in Trancoso nicht haben:
Das Hotel da Praça steht am Quadrado, dem Hauptplatz
der einstigen Jesuitensiedlung – früher war es auch unter
dem Namen Pousada do Quadrado bekannt. Die beiden
Architekten Bia Bittencourt und Ricardo Salem haben es
im September 2006 neu und vollkommen als Hommage
an die Kunst und Kultur von Trancoso gestaltet. Fast alle
Möbel sowie Accessoires sind Entwürfe einheimischer
Handwerker und Designer – sie richteten die luftigen
Räume mit massiven Hölzern und Naturfasern, Stoffen
im fröhlichen Streifenlook und bunt bemalten Fliesen ein.
Keines der elf Zimmer gleicht dem anderen – wer ganz
besonders private Ferien verbringen möchte, kann das
schlicht-charmante Beach House direkt am Sandstrand
mieten. Der Natur ganz nahe sind die Gäste auch in den
Gärten des Hotels da Praça, die dank jahrhundertealter
Bäume und exotischer Pflanzen wie ein verwunschener
Dschungel wirken. Eine kleine Überraschung wartet im
Restaurant Japaiano: Hier wird die traditionelle Küche
Bahias mit japanischen Spezialitäten zu einer raffinierten
Fusion Cuisine verbunden – Kreationen wie das Sushi de
Moqueca schmecken ungewöhnlich, aber ausgezeichnet.
Nach der kulinarischen Weltreise erreicht man das pure
Trancoso dann wieder in der Bar und lässt den Abend bei
Drinks sowie Musik aus Bahia ausklingen.
**Buchtipp: »Dona Flor und ihre zwei Ehemänner« von
Jorge Amado**

Bahia de tous les sens

Il n'existe pas de meilleure adresse à Trancoso : l'Hotel da
Praça – autrefois également connu sous le nom de Pousada
do Quadrado – se trouve sur le Quadrado, la place principale
de l'ancienne colonie de jésuites. En septembre 2006, les
deux architectes Bia Bittencourt et Ricardo Salem l'ont
entièrement redécoré, en hommage à l'art et à la civilisation
de Trancoso. Presque tous les meubles et accessoires sont
la création d'artisans et de designers autochtones – ils
aménagèrent les espaces aérés de bois massifs et de fibres
naturelles, de tissus à rayures éclatantes et de carrelages
multicolores. Aucune des onze chambres ne ressemble à sa
voisine – le touriste en quête de vacances tout individuelles
peut louer sur la plage de sable fin le Beach House, villa
de plage à la fois simple et charmante. Dans les jardins de
l'Hotel da Praça dont les arbres séculaires et la flore exotique
ressemblent à une jungle féerique, les visiteurs sont aussi
tout près de la nature. Une surprise les attend au restaurant
Japaiano : cuisine traditionnelle de Bahia et spécialités
japonaises fusionnent en une cuisine raffinée – des créations
comme le Sushi de Moqueca ont un goût certes inhabituel,
mais exquis. Après le tour du monde culinaire, l'on retrouve
à nouveau au bar le Trancoso authentique avant de terminer
la soirée par un drink au son de la musique de Bahia.
**Livre à emporter : « Dona Flor et ses deux maris » de
Jorge Amado**

ANREISE	40 Kilometer südlich des Internationalen Flughafens Porto Seguro gelegen. Transfer per Fähre (Porto Seguro-Arraial d'Ajuda) und Auto oder nur per Auto
PREISE	$$
ZIMMER	8 Apartments, 2 Suiten, 1 Beach House
KÜCHE	Japanische Gerichte mit brasilianischem Touch im Restaurant Japaiano
GESCHICHTE	Aus der ehemaligen Pousada do Quadrado wurde 2006 das Hotel da Praça
X-FAKTOR	Wohnen im neuen alten Stil Bahias

ACCÈS	Situé à 40 kilomètres au sud de l'aéroport international de Porto Seguro. Transfert par ferry (Porto Seguro-Arraial d'Ajuda) et voiture ou seulement par voiture
PRIX	$$
CHAMBRES	8 appartements, 2 suites, 1 Beach House
RESTAURATION	Cuisine japonaise avec un accent brésilien au Restaurant Japaiano
HISTOIRE	L'ancienne Pousada do Quadrado est devenue l'Hotel da Praça en 2006
LE « PETIT PLUS »	Le charme du vieux Bahia

Blue peace and tranquillity...
Estrela d'Água, Bahia

Blue peace and tranquillity

Trancoso has always been a place of refuge. The small town was founded in the mid-16th century by Jesuits wanting to afford the indigenous peoples some protection from the colonial conquerors. In the Seventies the hippies and drop-outs discovered it, finding in this tranquil settlement be-tween the ocean and the rain forest the perfect antidote to the bustle of São Paulo. And then there were the artists, seek-ing inspiration in the light and magic of this coast. Travel-lers can find happiness here too. Trancoso has miles of per-fect beaches, among the finest in all Brazil, and it also has the Estrela d'Água – a Pousada that is virtually paradise. Right on the famous Praia dos Nativos in grounds of 23,000 square metres (247,500 square feet) studded with palms and pink hibiscus, it has suites and chalets with all the cheery charm of the Bahia. To gaze at the pool and the ocean is to discover whole new unguessed-at shades of blue. You stroll down steps with gleaming red or blue rails, relax on turquoise sofas, and recline on cushions patterned with sun-yellow flowers. But there's no risk of colour overkill, thanks to the quiet tonalities of the understated interiors – dark par-quet and dark wood, plain lines and plain materials, lots of room and plenty of space. If anywhere could possibly be bet-ter to relax than the hammock, it can only be the spacious veranda, dappled by sunlight through the roof that leaves magical patterns of stripes on the seats and recliners. And if you really do need movement, there are fitness or yoga classes, a tennis court close by, or of course the blue Atlantic to go diving in.

Book to pack: "The Brazilians" by Joseph A. Page

Estrela d'Água	
Estrada Arraial d'Ajuda-Trancoso	
Trancoso – Porto Seguro	
Bahia	
Brazil	
CEP 45 818000	
Tel. (55) 7336681030	
E-mail: reservas@estreladagua.com.br	
Website: www.estreladagua.com.br	
www.great-escapes-hotels.com	

DIRECTIONS	Situated 40 km/25 miles south of Porto Seguro internatio-nal airport. Transfer by ferry (Porto Seguro-Arrial d'Ajuda) and road or by road only. There is a heliport 10 km/6 miles from the hotel
RATES	$$
ROOMS	14 suites, 2 master suites, 2 chalets
FOOD	The restaurant has a dream veranda and serves mainly regional cuisine
HISTORY	A beach resort in a former drop-out heaven
X-FACTOR	The colours are simply unbelievable!

Blaue Pause

Ein Fluchtpunkt war Trancoso schon immer: Mitte des
16. Jahrhunderts gründeten Jesuiten den kleinen Ort am
Atlantik, um den Indianern Schutz vor den Kolonialherren
zu bieten, in den 70ern kamen die Aussteiger und Hippies,
die in der Kolonie zwischen Meer und Regenwald Abstand
zum lauten Leben von São Paulo suchten, und schließlich
die Künstler, die sich von Licht und Magie der Küste Inspiration erhofften. Auch Reisende können hier ihr Glück finden: Trancoso besitzt kilometerlange Traumstrände, die zu
den schönsten Brasiliens gehören, und die Estrela d'Água –
eine Pousada wie ein Paradies. Direkt an der berühmten
Praia dos Nativos und auf 23.000 m² voller Palmen und
pink leuchtendem Hibiskus gelegen, besitzt sie Suiten und
Chalets mit dem fröhlichen Charme von Bahia. Der Blick
auf Pool und Meer erweitert die Farbpalette »blau« um nie
geahnte Nuancen, man läuft Treppen mit strahlend rot
oder blau gestrichenem Geländer hinauf, entspannt auf tür-
kisfarbenen Sofas und lehnt in Kissen mit sonnengelben
Blumenmotiven. Dafür, dass die vielen Farbtupfer keine
Farbblindheit verursachen, sorgt das ansonsten reduzierte
Interiordesign – dunkles Parkett und Holz, einfache Linien
und einfache Materialien, viel Raum und viel Weite. Schöner
als in der Hängematte lässt es sich vielleicht nur noch auf
der großen Veranda entspannen, durch deren Dach die Son-
nenstrahlen fallen und Streifenmuster auf Sitzgruppen und
Liegen zaubern. Wer sich unter allen Umständen bewegen
will, nimmt Fitness- oder Yogastunden, spielt eine Runde
Tennis auf dem nahen Court oder taucht einfach im Blau
des Atlantiks ab.

Buchtipp: »Brasilien, Brasilien« von João Ubaldo Ribeiro

L'heure bleue

Transoco a été fondé par les jésuites au milieu du 16e siècle
pour recueillir les Indiens persécutés par les coloniaux. Des
amoureux de la nature et de la paix qui cherchaient entre
l'océan et la forêt tropicale un endroit à l'écart de São Paulo
la trépidante, l'ont redécouvert au cours des années 70, et
finalement des artistes en quête d'inspiration et attirés par
la lumière et la magie de la côte sont venus s'y installer.
Trancoso possède aussi, pour le plus grand bonheur des
voyageurs, des kilomètres de fin sable blanc et de cocotiers,
les plus belles plages du Brésil, et une pousada paradisiaque.
L'Estrela d'Água, c'est son nom, est située sur la célèbre
Praia dos Nativos. Sur 23.000 mètres carrés plantés de palmiers et d'hibiscus flamboyants, elle propose des suites et
des chalets qui possèdent le charme enjoué et nonchalant
de Bahia. La plage et l'océan offrent des tons de bleus incon-
nus, les rampes des escaliers sont peintes en bleu ou rouge
vif, les canapés turquoise et des coussins aux motifs de tour-
nesols ensoleillés invitent à la détente. L'œil peut se reposer
de ces splendeurs bariolées dans les intérieurs au design
plus sobre – parquets et bois sombres, lignes et matériaux
simples, beaucoup d'espace et de place. On peut aussi
délaisser le hamac pour la grande véranda et regarder les
rayons du soleil dessiner des rayures sur les fauteuils et les
divans. Celui qui veut vraiment faire de l'exercice peut
s'adonner au programme de remise en forme ou prendre
des cours de yoga, jouer un moment au tennis sur le court
tout proche ou plonger tête première dans le grand bleu.

**Livre à emporter : « Vive le peuple brésilien »
de João Ubaldo Ribeiro**

ANREISE	40 Kilometer südlich des Internationalen Flughafens Porto Seguro gelegen, Transfer per Fähre (Porto Seguro-Arrial d'Ajuda) und Auto oder nur per Auto. Ein Heliport ist 10 Kilometer vom Hotel entfernt
PREISE	$$
ZIMMER	14 Suiten, 2 Master Suiten, 2 Chalets
KÜCHE	Im Restaurant mit Traumveranda wird vor allem regionale Küche serviert
GESCHICHTE	Strandresort im ehemaligen Aussteigerparadies
X-FAKTOR	Alles so schön bunt hier!

ACCÈS	Situé à 40 kilomètres au sud de l'aéroport internatio-nal de Porto Seguro, transfert par ferry (Porto Seguro-Arrial d'Ajuda) et par voiture. Un héliport se trouve à 10 kilomètres de l'hôtel
PRIX	$$
CHAMBRES	14 suites, 2 Master Suites, 2 chalets
RESTAURATION	Le restaurant propose des spécialités régionales
HISTOIRE	Hôtel de plage, autrefois le paradis de ceux qui avaient tout laissé derrière eux
LE « PETIT PLUS »	Des couleurs enchanteresses !

Our little realm...
Pousada Etnia, Bahia

Our little realm

There are times when your ticket quite clearly reads "Porto Seguro, Brazil" – and all the same you land in the oriental world of the Arabian Nights, or on the shores of the Mediterranean. In fact you're on vacation at the Pousada Etnia, a charming retreat tucked away in a dreamy Trancoso park. It entirely lives up to its name, and the bungalows are conceived in homage to a variety of places and cultures. The "Trancoso" is the bungalow closest in feel to the Brazilian setting. It is simply furnished with rattan armchairs, native wood, and light-hued fabrics, and its understated grace sets off the exuberance of the outside world on the doorstep all the more. Dark furniture reminiscent of colonial times, animal prints, and African-inspired art are the hallmark of the "Tribal" bungalow, with its discreet safari mood. In the "Cottage" you can enjoy the bright and breezy style of tropical islands such as the Seychelles, with just a hint of the English south. If other European moods are what you crave, relax in the "Mediterráneo" on the blue-and-white cushions and marvel at the model sailing ships. Finally, all the magic of the Orient is yours in the "Maroccos" bungalow with its typical pointed doors, the golden gleam of brass, and hand-woven carpets. The proprietors of Etnia aim to transcend borders and create a cosmopolitan kaleidoscope where the best of various cultures is juxtaposed and possesses a new fascination in the encounter. The hotel shop sells antiques and art to match the styles – and throws in a boundless enthusiasm for the Pousada philosophy for free.

Book to pack: "Brazil" by John Updike

Pousada Etnia
CX.P. 142
Trancoso – Porto Seguro
Bahia, Brazil
CEP 45818 000
Tel. (55) 7336681137
Fax (55) 736681549
E-mail: etniabrasil@etniabrasil.com.br
Website: www.etniabrasil.com.br
www.great-escapes-hotels.com

DIRECTIONS	Situated 40 km/25 miles south of Porto Seguro international airport. Transfer by ferry (Porto Seguro-Arrial d'Ajuda) and road or by road only
RATES	$
ROOMS	8 Bungalows
FOOD	Light cuisine in the poolside restaurant. The bar is famed for its drinks
HISTORY	Opened in December 2002
X-FACTOR	A meeting place for the world's cultures

Unsere kleine Welt

Manchmal steht auf dem Flugschein ganz deutlich »Porto Seguro, Brasilien« – und man landet doch in tausendund-einer Nacht des Orients oder an den Gestaden des Mittel-meers ... Dann nämlich, wenn man seinen Urlaub in der Pousada Etnia verbringt, einer charmanten Anlage mitten in einem verwunschenen Park von Trancoso. Sie macht ihrem Namen alle Ehre und hat die Bungalows als Hommage an unterschiedliche Destinationen und Kulturen entworfen. Der brasilianischen Umgebung am nächsten ist der Bungalow »Trancoso«, das schlicht mit Rattansesseln, ein-heimischem Holz und hellen Stoffen eingerichtet ist und dank seiner Zurückhaltung die üppige Natur vor der Tür nur noch besser zur Geltung bringt. Dunkle und an Kolo-nialzeiten erinnernde Möbel, Animalprints und afrikanische inspirierte Kunst zeichnen die Wohnung »Tribal« aus und sorgen für dezentes Safari-Feeling; das luftige Flair tropi-scher Inseln wie der Seychellen, gemischt mit einem Hauch Südengland, herrscht im »Cottage«. Wer sich nach weiteren europäischen Einflüssen sehnt, zieht in die Unterkunft »Mediterrâneo« und entspannt dort auf blau-weiß-gestreifen Kissen oder bewundert Segelschiff-Modelle. Die Magie des Orients schließlich besitzt der Bungalow »Maroccos« – mit den typischen, spitz zulaufenden Türen, goldglänzendem Messing und handgewebten Teppichen. Es geht den Besit-zern von Etnia darum, Grenzen aufzuheben und ein kos-mopolitisches Kaleidoskop zu schaffen, in dem das Beste aus verschiedenen Kulturkreisen unvermittelt aufeinander trifft und gerade deshalb so faszinierend ist. Im hoteleige-nen Shop werden passende Antiquitäten und Kunst verkauft – die Begeisterung für die Philosophie der Pousada gibt es gratis mit dazu.

Buchtipp: »Brasilien« von John Updike

Citoyens du monde

On peut très bien lire « Porto Seguro, Brésil » sur le billet d'avion et se retrouver dans une ambiance de Mille et Une Nuits ou sur les rivages de la Méditerranée... C'est ce qui arrive si l'on passe ses vacances a la Pousada Etnia, un hôtel charmant situé dans un parc ravissant à Trancoso. Son nom est tout un programme et, de fait, les bungalows ont été conçus et décorés en hommage à divers pays et cultures. Le bungalow « Trancoso » se rapproche le plus de l'environnement brésilien avec ses fauteuils de rotin, ses essences locales et ses étoffes claires – sa sobriété met en valeur la végétation exubérante qui s'épanouit au pied de la porte. Le bungalow « Tribal », quant à lui, est doté de meubles sombres évoquant l'ère coloniale, d'impressions animalières et d'œuvres inspirées de l'art africain. Le « Cottage » marie l'atmosphère des îles heureuses et des accents cosy du sud anglais. Celui qui désire d'autres influences européennes s'installe dans le bungalow « Me-diterrâneo », se détend sur des coussins rayés bleu et blanc ou admire des maquettes de voiliers. Et enfin le bungalow « Maroccos » avec ses portes en ogive, ses laitons étincelants et ses tapis tissés à la main offre toute la magie de l'Orient. Les propriétaires d'Etnia veulent abolir les frontières et créer une mosaïque cosmopolite réunissant le meilleur de ce que les diverses cultures ont à offrir, et cette rencontre est fascinante. La boutique de l'hôtel vend les antiquités et les œuvres d'art correspondants – l'enthousiasme pour la philosophie qui règne en ces lieux est gracieusement offert en sus.

Livre à emporter : « Brésil » de John Updike

ANREISE	40 Kilometer südlich des Internationalen Flughafens Porto Seguro gelegen. Transfer per Fähre (Porto Seguro-Arrial d'Ajuda) und Auto oder nur per Auto
PREISE	$
ZIMMER	8 Bungalows
KÜCHE	Leichte Küche am Pool-Restaurant. Die Bar ist für ihre Drinks berühmt
GESCHICHTE	Im Dezember 2002 eröffnet
X-FAKTOR	Ein Treffpunkt der Kulturen

ACCÈS	Situé à 40 kilomètres au sud de l'aéroport internatio-nal de Porto Seguro. Transfert par ferry (Porto Seguro-Arrial d'Ajuda) et voiture ou seulement par voiture
PRIX	$
CHAMBRES	8 bungalows
RESTAURATION	Cuisine légère au restaurant de la piscine. Le bar est renommé pour ses cocktails
HISTOIRE	Ouvert en décembre 2002
LE « PETIT PLUS »	Le rendez-vous des cultures

The discovery of solitude...
Ponta do Camarão, Bahia

The discovery of solitude

If you make the journey to Caraíva, you can leave the trunk behind and travel light. "Flip-flops, tennis shoes, shorts, T-shirts, swimming gear, a sun hat, suntan lotion, and money" – that is all the Caraíva website recommends visitors bring with them. Caraíva is tucked away on the south coast of Bahia, cut off by the ocean on the one side and the river on the other. There are no surfaced roads, no cars, no electricity. And nonetheless the village offers sheer luxury: the discovery of solitude, closeness to nature, and the exclusive bungalows of Ponta do Camarão amid the greenery, with a view so gloriously close to kitsch it rivals any picture postcard. The turquoise of the water is taken up in the colour the walls are painted, and the sunlight is echoed in the yellow door frames and orange valances. A maximum of four guests at a time are spoilt rotten by Fernanda and Flavio. Revel in being the master, for a time, of this bright and spacious house. At the thermal pool you can enjoy massages with natural oils or relax in a mineral bath. And every day you can order the choicest of fare – Flavio's fish is sheer poetry, and the home-baked bread is to die for. On a day that begins in this paradise, everything's bound to be perfect. Take a walk by Satu Lagoon, for instance, and drink cool coconut milk straight from the coconut at the plantation. If you like boats, explore a whole new world of rain forest and mangroves on the Rio Caraíva, or if fishing is your preference you can go in search of supper. No one here bothers with travel agents – all you need do is have a word with your amiable hosts, or one of the fishermen on the beach, and ask for their tips. But do be sure to plan your evenings. Keep the hours of darkness free for gazing out from your Ponta do Camarão bungalow – the night sky over Caraíva is truly awash with stars.

Book to pack: "By the River Piedra I sat down and wept" by Paulo Coelho

Ponta do Camarão
between Praia do Espelho and Caraíva
Bahia
Brazil
Tel. (55) 1130629200
E-mail: info@espelhodamaravilha.com
No website. Ponta do Camarão can be found at: www.espelhodamaravilha.com.br/b_camarao.htm
www.great-escapes-hotels.com

DIRECTIONS	Situated 115 km/72 miles south of Porto Seguro airport. The two-hour road transfer is organised. The final stretch, by river, is done by canoe
RATES	$$$$
ROOMS	2 Bungalows for 2 people (each offering 100 square metres/1,076 square feet of accommodation)
FOOD	Brazilian cuisine with a hint of the oriental. Proprietor Flavio likes to cook fish and to prepare the food according to his guests' personal wishes
HISTORY	Opened in October 2002
X-FACTOR	Definitely an insider tip

Die Entdeckung der Einsamkeit

Wer nach Caraíva reist, kann den Schrankkoffer getrost zu
Hause lassen. »Flip Flops, Tennisschuhe, Shorts, T-Shirts,
Badesachen, Sonnenhut, Sonnencreme und Geld« – das
ist alles, was die ortseigene Website künftigen Gästen an
Gepäck empfiehlt. Caraíva versteckt sich an der Südküste
von Bahia, isoliert vom Ozean auf der einen und dem Fluss
auf der anderen Seite, ohne asphaltierte Straßen, ohne
Autos, ohne Strom. Und dennoch bietet das Dorf Luxus:
die Entdeckung der Einsamkeit, die Nähe zur Natur und die
exklusiven Bungalows von Ponta do Camarão – im Grünen
gelegen und mit einer Aussicht so kitschig-schön wie eine
Fototapete. Das Türkisblau des Wassers spiegelt sich in der
Wandfarbe wieder und das Sonnenlicht in den gelben Tür-
rahmen und Einfassungen sowie den orangefarbenen
Volants. Maximal vier Personen genießen hier das Verwöhn-
programm von Fernanda und Flavio: Sie sind Herren auf
Zeit über ein helles Haus mit fast 100m², können sich im
Thermalbad mit natürlichen Ölen massieren lassen oder
im Salzbad entspannen und sich jeden Tag ihr Leibgericht
wünschen – Flavios Fisch ist ein Gedicht, und ins selbst
gebackene Brot möchte man sich am liebsten hineinlegen.
An Tagen, die in diesem Paradies beginnen, kann eigentlich
nichts mehr schief gehen. Man spaziert z. B. an der Lagune
von Satu entlang und trinkt bei der kleinen Plantage kühle
Kokosmilch frisch aus der Nuss. Bootsfreunde schippern
auf dem Rio Caraíva durch Regenwald und Mangroven in
eine andere Welt, und Angler machen sich geduldig auf die
Suche nach ihrem Abendessen. Reiseagenturen braucht hier
niemand – es reicht vollkommen aus, die liebenswerten
Gastgeber oder einen der Fischer am Strand anzusprechen
und um die besten Tipps zu bitten. Nur den Abend sollte
man fest planen und vor den Bungalows von Ponta do
Camarão einfach in die Nacht schauen – der Himmel über
Caraíva ist ein Sternenmeer.
**Buchtipp: »Am Ufer des Rio Piedra saß ich und weinte«
von Paulo Coelho**

La découverte de la solitude

Celui qui se rend à Caraíva, n'a pas besoin d'emmener de
grosses valises. «Tongs, tennis, t-shirts, shorts, maillots de
bain, chapeau, crème solaire et de l'argent», voilà ce qu'on
peut lire sur le site web de Caraíva. Caraíva est niché sur la
côte sud de Bahia, isolé du reste du monde par l'Océan d'un
côté et par le fleuve de l'autre, sans route goudronnée, sans
voitures ni électricité. Et pourtant le village offre un luxe qui
n'a pas de prix : la découverte de la solitude, la proximité de
la nature et les bungalows de Ponta do Camarão absolument
uniques dans leur genre – avec la végétation luxuriante qui
les entoure et leur vue digne d'une carte postale. Le bleu
turquoise de l'eau se reflète sur les murs et la lumière du
soleil, dans les encadrements jaunes de portes et de fenêtre
ainsi que dans les étoffes orangées. Quatre personnes au
maximum peuvent se laisser choyer ici par Fernanda et
Flavio. Résidant dans une demeure claire de près de 100
mètres carrés, les clients peuvent se faire masser avec des
huiles naturelles ou se détendre dans un bain de sel marin.
Ils peuvent aussi commander tous les jours leur plat favori,
le poisson préparé par Flavio est un poème et son pain maison, un vrai régal. Les jours passés dans ce paradis sont des
moments de rêve. On peut se promener par exemple le long
du lagon de Satu et boire un lait de coco bien frais dans la
petite plantation. Les amoureux du bateau descendront le
Rio Caraíva à travers la forêt tropicale et les mangroves, les
pêcheurs attendront avec patience que leur repas du soir
frétille au bout de la ligne. Il suffit de demander à l'hôte
plein de gentillesse quels sont ses meilleurs tuyaux. Mais
n'entreprenez rien le soir, contentez-vous de regarder
l'obscurité devant les bungalows de Ponta do Camarão –
le ciel étoilé au-dessus de Caraíva est une splendeur.
**Livre à emporter : « Sur le bord de la rivière Piedra »
de Paulo Coelho**

ANREISE	115 Kilometer südlich des Flughafens von Porto Seguro gelegen. Zweistündiger Transfer per Auto wird organisiert. Das letzte Stück über den Fluss legt man im Kanu zurück
PREISE	$$$$
ZIMMER	2 Bungalows für je 2 Personen (je 100 Quadratmeter Wohnfläche)
KÜCHE	Brasilianische Küche mit leicht orientalischem Touch. Besitzer Flavio kocht viel Fisch und ganz nach persön- lichem Geschmack der Gäste
GESCHICHTE	Im Oktober 2002 eröffnet
X-FAKTOR	Ein Geheimtipp

ACCÈS	Situé à 115 kilomètres au sud de l'aéroport de Porto Seguro. Le transfert en voiture (deux heures) est orga- nisé. La dernière partie sur le fleuve se fait en canoë
PRIX	$$$$
CHAMBRES	2 bungalows pour 2 Personen (de 100 mètres carrés chacun)
CUISINE	Cuisine brésilienne avec une légère note orientale. Le propriétaire Flavio cuisine beaucoup de plats à base de poisson et tient compte des goûts de ses clients
HISTOIRE	Ouvert depuis octobre 2002
LE « PETIT PLUS »	Une adresse à garder pour soi

A hidden paradise...
Vila Naiá – Paralelo 17°, Bahia

A hidden paradise

This paradise isn't one with an address. There's no zip code,
no streeet name, no house number. No guidebook or map
will help you find it – to get to Vila Naiá, you need the sixth
sense for orientation that a pilot, rally driver, or helmsman
has. It's a small resort, opened only in September 2004, on
the Atlantic coast near Corumbau, on the edge of the Monte
Pascoal National Park and a fishing reservation where only
the indigenous population are allowed out to sea. Bahia,
otherwise so temperamental, seems worlds away. All you can
hear is the breeze in the palm fronds and the wavelets lap-
ping on the beach. The air you breathe has a mild salty tang,
and the sun is warm on your skin. For ten years, architect
Renato Marques and owner Renata Mellão worked at the Vila
Naiá concept, till the buildings were as plain and true to the
local spirit as the natural world all around – not too much
the ecological resort, and not too understated on the luxuries
for guests who like their creature comforts. The four apartments and four houses are simple of line, panelled in dark
wood within, and not over-furnished. The only strong
colours added to the natural hues are the chairs, hammocks
and throws. The kitchen is a no-frills affair as well. At Vila
Naiá, Maria Alice Solimene prepares typical Brazilian specialities and plans her menu to fit the fishermen's catch that
morning and according to what the garden provides. Those
with even more purist tastes can eat at Rafael Rosa, where
the manager and second maitre is probably the only chef in
the country to be serving "raw living food".

Book to pack: "Captains of the Sands" by Jorge Amado

Vila Naiá – Paralelo 17°
Corumbau
Bahia
Brazil
Tel. (55) 7335731006 and (55) 7332943881
E-mail: reservas@vilanaia.com.br
Website: www.vilanaia.com.br
www.great-escapes-hotels.com

DIRECTIONS	Situated 60 km/38 miles south of Porto Seguro airport. Transfer by light aircraft (20 minutes, US$ 323), Landrover (approx. 4 hours, US$ 145) or Landrover and boat (2 hours 45 minutes, US$ 340)
RATES	$$
ROOMS	4 apartments for 2 persons, 4 houses for 3 persons
FOOD	Brazilian cuisine and "raw living food"
HISTORY	Ten years in the making, it opened in 2004
X-FACTOR	Right in the heart of nature

Das versteckte Paradies

Das Paradies hat keine genaue Adresse – keine Straße, keine Hausnummer, keine Postleitzahl. Bei seiner Entdeckung nützt kein Reiseführer und keine Landkarte – wer zur Vila Naiá möchte, muss dem Orientierungssinn des Piloten, Fahrers oder Bootsmannes vertrauen. Das kleine, erst im September 2004 eröffnete Resort liegt an der Atlantikküste bei Corumbau; am Rand des Nationalparks Monte Pascoal und eines Fischreservats, in dem nur die Einheimischen hinaus aufs Meer fahren dürfen. Hier scheint das sonst so temperamentvolle Bahia Welten entfernt zu sein; man hört den Wind in den Palmen und die Wellen an den Strand rauschen, atmet salzig-sanfte Luft und spürt die Sonne auf der Haut. Zehn Jahre lang haben Architekt Renato Marques und Besitzerin Renata Mellão am Konzept der Vila Naiá getüftelt, bis die Häuser genau so schlicht und ursprünglich wie die umliegende Natur waren, nicht zu sehr in Richtung »Öko-Resort« abdrifteten und nicht zu wenig Luxus für anspruchsvolle Gäste bieten. Die vier Apartments und vier Häuser wurden innen mit dunklem Holz verkleidet und zeigen einfache Linien und sparsame Möblierung – einige bunte Stühle, Hängematten und Decken sind die einzigen Akzente inmitten der Naturtöne. Ohne Schnörkel kommt auch die Küche aus: In der Vila Naiá kocht Maria Alice Solimene typisch brasilianische Spezialitäten und richtet ihre Menükarte danach aus, was die Fischer jeden Morgen anliefern oder der hauseigene Biogarten hergibt. Wer es noch puristischer mag, sollte bei Rafael Rosa essen: Der Manager der Anlage und zugleich ihr zweiter Maître serviert als wahrscheinlich einziger Küchenchef des Landes »raw living food«, ausschließlich rohe und naturbelassene Gerichte.

Buchtipp: »Herren des Strandes« von Jorge Amado

Un paradis caché

Le paradis n'a pas d'adresse – pas de rue, pas de numéro, pas de code postal. Pour le découvrir, les guides et les cartes ne servent à rien. Celui qui veut se rendre à la Vila Naiá doit se fier au sens de l'orientation du pilote d'avion, du chauffeur de voiture ou du capitaine de bateau. Le petit hôtel, ouvert seulement depuis septembre 2004, se trouve sur la côte atlantique près de Corumbau, en bordure du parc national de Monte Pascoal et d'une réserve maritime où seuls les autochtones ont le droit de pénétrer. La ville trépidante de Bahia semble à des années-lumière. Ici on entend le murmure du vent dans les palmiers et le grondement des vagues sur la plage, on respire l'air marin et l'on sent la caresse du soleil sur sa peau. Pendant dix ans, l'architecte Renato Marques et la propriétaire Renata Mellão ont travaillé sur le concept de la Vila Naiá, jusqu'à ce que les maisons soient aussi simples et authentiques que la nature environnante, sans tomber dans l'écologie à outrance mais en offrant assez de luxe pour les clients exigeants. Les quatre appartements et les quatre maisons habillés de bois sombre ont des lignes sobres et sont décorés sans exubérance – les chaises, hamacs et couvertures sont les seuls accents de couleur parmi les tons naturels. La cuisine est elle aussi dénuée de fioritures : à la Vila Naiá, Maria Alice Solimene prépare des spécialités typiquement brésiliennes en fonction des poissons que lui apportent les pêcheurs tous les matins ou en fonction des produits du jardin bio. Si vous êtes encore plus puriste, ne manquez pas d'aller manger chez Rafael Rosa : le gérant de l'hôtel, qui est en même temps le deuxième maître queux, est probablement le seul chef du pays à servir une « raw living food », des plats exclusivement crus et naturels.

Livre à emporter : « Capitaines des sables » de Jorge Amado

ANREISE	60 Kilometer südlich des Flughafens Porto Seguro gelegen. Transfer per Kleinflugzeug (20 Minuten, US$ 323), Landrover (4 Stunden, US$ 145) oder Landrover und Boot (2 Stunden 45 Minuten, US$ 340)
PREISE	$$
ZIMMER	4 Apartments für max. 2 Personen, 4 Häuser für max. 3 Personen
KÜCHE	Brasilianische Gerichte und »raw living food«
GESCHICHTE	Nach zehnjähriger Entwicklung 2004 eröffnet
X-FAKTOR	Im Herzen der Natur

ACCÈS	Situé à 60 kilomètres au sud de l'aéroport de Porto Seguro. Transfer en petit avion (20 minutes, US$ 323), en Landrover (env. 4 heures, US$ 145) ou en Landrover et en bateau (2 heures 45 minutes, US$ 340)
PRIX	$$
CHAMBRES	4 appartements pour 2 personnes au maximum, 4 maisons pour 3 personnes au maximum
RESTAURATION	Plats brésiliens et « raw living food »
HISTOIRE	Ouvert en 2004 après une conception de dix ans
LE « PETIT PLUS »	On ne saurait être encore plus proche de la nature

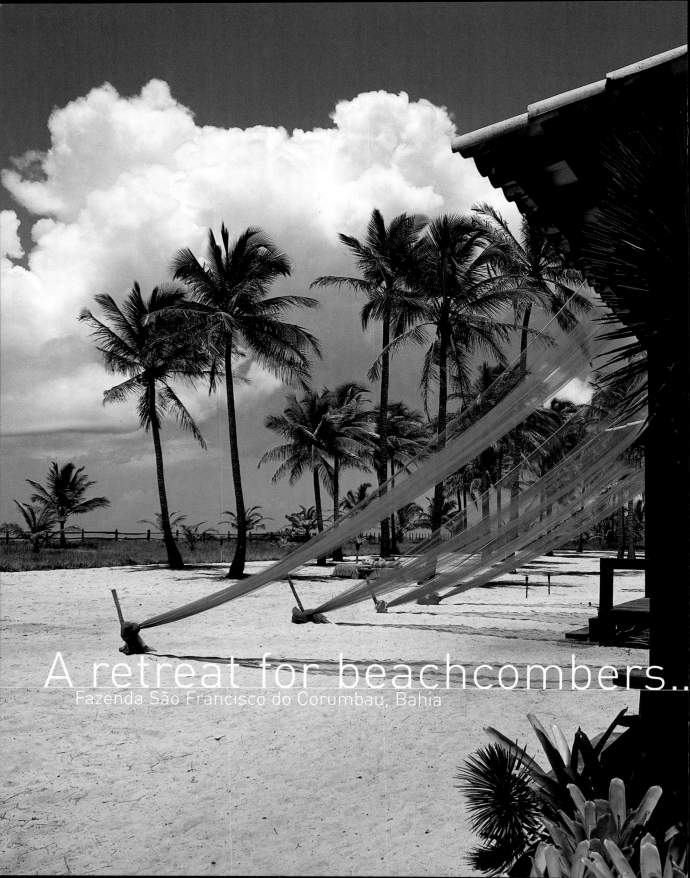

A retreat for beachcombers..
Fazenda São Francisco do Corumbau, Bahia

A retreat for beachcombers

Bahia may be one of the liveliest, most temperamental of Brazil's federal states, but it also honours the principle of the laid-back, leisurely pace. Whether at the office, in the supermarket, or on the street, no one gets hot under the collar if they can help it, and the local saying even has it that anyone running in Bahia must be either a thief or someone who's lost something important beyond belief. The lightness of being is especially infectious if you visit the south of the region, where the country is flat as a pancake and the white beaches and palm groves reach right to the horizon. You'll forget the very concept of "stress" the moment you dig your toes into the sand, pick up your first coconut, or simply feel the salt water tingle on your skin. To be a guest at the Fazenda São Francisco do Corumbau is to slip into a time capsule – your alarm clock, watch, and mobile phone may as well stay in the suitcase. The estate, located between Porto Seguro and Prado, was formerly a coconut plantation; but for roughly the last 20 years the 5,000 or so palms have simply been a dream backdrop, and a perfect contrast to the white sand. The eight suites are a rich composition in colour, with exotic blooms on the sofa cushions, red drapes hung before lime-green walls, shower curtains in every tropical colour of your dreams, and bold tartan bedspreads to make even a Scotsman envious. The Fazenda has a fish restaurant and a first-rate programme of sporting options, making it truly a place to chill and enjoy – a feelgood retreat to savour to the full.

Book to pack: "Macunaíma" by Mario de Andrade

Fazenda São Francisco do Corumbau		
Ponta do Corumbau		
Bahia		
Brazil		
Tel. (55) 7332942250 and (55) 1130784411		
E-mail: reservas@corumbau.com.br		
Website: www.corumbau.com.br		
www.great-escapes-hotels.com		
	DIRECTIONS	Situated between Porto Seguro and Prado, 1,000 km/ 625 miles north of Rio de Janeiro. The transfer from Porto Seguro is organised (Landrover for 6 people: US$ 145 or helicopter for 3 people: US$ 385)
	RATES	$$
	ROOMS	10 suites (6 in the main building, 4 in bungalows)
	FOOD	Fresh fish and Brazilian specialities
	HISTORY	In the 80s, a coconut plantation was made over into a small hotel
	X-FACTOR	A vacation as peaceful as it gets

Für Strandläufer

Bahia gehört zu den temperamentvollsten Bundesstaaten
Brasiliens, doch zugleich macht man hier die Gelassenheit
und Langsamkeit zum Lebensprinzip. Egal, ob im Büro,
im Supermarkt oder auf der Straße – niemand lässt sich so
leicht aus der Ruhe bringen, und die Einheimischen be-
haupten sogar, wer in Bahia renne, sei entweder ein Dieb
oder müsse gerade etwas unglaublich Wichtiges verloren
haben. Von der Leichtigkeit des Seins lassen sich Besucher
vor allem im Süden der Region anstecken; dort, wo das
Land wie flachgebügelt daliegt und sich weiße Strände und
Palmenhaine bis hinter den Horizont ziehen. Begriffe wie
»Stress« oder »Hektik« tilgt man in dem Moment aus seinem Wortschatz, in dem man zum ersten Mal die Füße im
Sand vergräbt, die erste Kokosnuss vom Boden aufhebt oder
den ersten Spritzer Salzwasser auf der Haut spürt. Die Fazenda São Francisco do Corumbau schenkt ihren Gästen
Ferien wie in einem Zeitloch – Wecker, Armbanduhren oder
Handys bleiben wie von selbst im Koffer. Ursprünglich war
das Anwesen zwischen Porto Seguro und Prado eine Kokosplantage; seit rund 20 Jahren sind die 5.000 Palmen aber
nur noch Traumkulisse und perfekter Kontrast zum weißen
Strand. Für ordentlich Farbe wird in den acht Suiten gesorgt
– in den Räumen wachsen exotische Blumen auf den Sofa-
kissen, vor lindgrünen Wänden wehen rote Gardinen, die
Duschvorhänge sind so bunt wie ein Südseetraum, und auf
die großkarierten Bettdecken wären sogar Schotten neidisch.
Die Fazenda ist auch dank ihres Fischrestaurants und ihres
Sportprogramm ein echtes Gute-Laune-Ziel – und eines,
das man in aller Seelenruhe genießen kann.

Buchtipp: »Macunaíma« von Mario de Andrade

Eau, sable et cocotiers

Les Bahianais sont bien connus pour leur tempérament
fougueux, pourtant la tranquillité et la lenteur ont été éle-
vées ici en principes de vie. Au bureau, au supermarché ou
dans la rue, les gens perdent rarement leur sang-froid, et les
autochtones prétendent même que celui qui court à Bahia a
volé quelque chose ou perdu un objet auquel il tenait énor-
mément. Cette légèreté de l'être est contagieuse, surtout au
sud de la région, là où le pays semble plat et lisse, là où les
plages de sable blanc et les bosquets de cocotiers s'étirent
jusqu'à l'horizon.

Dès le moment où l'on plonge avec délice ses pieds dans
le sable fin, où l'on ramasse la première noix de coco et où
l'eau salée touche la peau, des mots comme « stress » et
« nervosité » disparaissent du vocabulaire. À la Fazenda
São Francisco do Corumbau, le temps n'existe plus – les
réveils, les montres et les portables restent dans les valises.
À l'origine la propriété située entre Porto Seguro et Prado
était une plantation de coprah : depuis une vingtaine d'années, un maison s'y élève et les 5.000 palmiers qui plantent
un décor de rêve se marient avec bonheur au sable blanc.
Ici la couleur est reine : à l'intérieur des suites, des fleurs
exotiques s'épanouissent sur les coussins des canapés, des
rideaux rouges se déploient sur des murs vert tilleul, les
rideaux de douche sont aussi colorés qu'un rêve des mers
du Sud et les Écossais apprécieraient sans aucun doute les
jetés de lit à grands carreaux. Avec son restaurant aux spécialités de poisson et son programme sportif, la Fazenda
est aussi un lieu où règne la bonne humeur – et on peut
s'y détendre en toute quiétude.

Livre à emporter : « Macunaíma » de Mario de Andrade

ANREISE	Zwischen Porto Seguro und Prado gelegen, 1.000 Kilo-meter nördlich von Rio de Janeiro. Transfer ab Porto Seguro wird organisiert (Landrover für 6 Personen: US$ 145 oder Helikopter für 3 Personen: US$ 385)
PREISE	$$
ZIMMER	10 Suiten (6 im Haupthaus, 4 in Bungalows)
KÜCHE	Frischer Fisch und brasilianische Spezialitäten
GESCHICHTE	Aus einer Kokosplantage wurde in den 80er Jahren ein kleines Hotel
X-FAKTOR	Ferien in aller Ruhe

ACCÈS	Situé entre Porto Seguro et Prado, à 1.000 kilomètres au nord de Rio de Janeiro. Le transfert est organisé à partir de Porto Seguro (Landrover pour 6 personnes : US$ 145 ou hélicoptère pour 3 personnes : US$ 385)
PRIX	$$
CHAMBRES	10 suites (6 dans la maison principale, 4 dans des bungalows)
RESTAURATION	Poisson frais et spécialités brésiliennes
HISTOIRE	Une plantation de cocotiers transformée en hôtel au cours des années 80
LE « PETIT PLUS »	Des vacances que rien ne peut troubler

A room with a view...
La Posada del Faro, Maldonado

A room with a view

East of Montevideo and Punta del Este lies the vacation capital of Uruguay: white sandy beaches lapped by the waves of the Atlantic and the River Plate, and small townships with all the necessary infrastructure of shops, restaurants, and clubs. Many are overrun in the high season – but one place that has so far remained relatively quiet is José Ignacio, about 30 kilometres or just under 20 miles from Punta del Este. The perfect retreat for a summer vacation is the Posada del Faro, with its gleaming white walls, awnings, and sun umbrellas. It's just 30 metres (100 feet) from the ocean, and the views it commands of the Atlantic would be fit for the cinema. The pool is the purest blue, and so (most days) is the sky; and if that's not enough blue for you, there are blue-painted doors or blue carpets here and there around the interior. Otherwise the ten rooms are cream-coloured, with a good deal of wood; every room is individually furnished, but they all have their own secluded terrace with recliners or hammocks. In the evenings when the barbecue is fired up for the typical "asado" and diners take their places at long tables, it's like eating with good friends. The Posada del Faro is an excellent base for local excursions – to bathing resorts such as Punta del Este or La Paloma, to the Isla de Lobos with its colony of sea lions, or to Cerro Catedral, which at 513 metres (just under 1,600 feet) is Uruguay's loftiest peak!

Book to pack: "Blood Pact & Other Stories" by Mario Benedetti

La Posada del Faro	
Calle de la Bahia esquina Timonel	
Faro de José Ignacio	
Maldonado	
Uruguay	
Tel. (598) 486 2110	
Fax (598) 486 2111	
E-mail: informacion@posadadelfaro.com	
Website: www.posadadelfaro.com	
www.great-escapes-hotels.com	

DIRECTIONS	Situated 30 km/19 miles northeast of Punta del Este, on the Atlantic coast
RATES	$$
ROOMS	10 individually furnished double rooms
FOOD	A small barbecue restaurant with a fine view of the ocean
HISTORY	A new retreat, alongside an old lighthouse dating from 1877
X-FACTOR	Like a private villa far from the madding crowd

Schöne Aussichten

Östlich von Montevideo und Punta del Este liegen Uruguays Urlaubsparadiese: weiße Sandstrände, an die die Wellen von Río de la Plata und Atlantik rollen, sowie kleine Orte mit der nötigen Infrastuktur aus Geschäften, Restaurants und Clubs. Viele sind während der Hochsaison überlaufen – zu den noch relativ ruhigen Zielen gehört José Ignacio, rund 30 Kilometer von Punta del Este entfernt. Hier verbringt man die schönste Sommerfrische in der Posada del Faro, die mit ihren strahlend weißen Mauern, Sonnensegeln und Sonnenschirmen gerade einmal 30 Meter vom Meer entfernt steht und kinotaugliche Atlantikansichten möglich macht. Ganz in Blau zeigen sich auch der Pool und (an den meisten Tagen) der Himmel; und wer von diesen Farbtönen nicht genug bekommt, findet auch im Haus die ein oder andere blau gestrichene Tür oder einen blauen Teppich. Ansonsten herrschen in den zehn Zimmern Cremetöne und viel Holz; jeder Raum ist unterschiedlich eingerichtet, aber alle besitzen eine eigene und geschützte Terrasse mit Liegestühlen oder Hängematten. Wie zu Gast bei guten Freunden fühlt man sich, wenn abends der Grill fürs typische »asado« angeheizt und an langen Tischen getafelt wird. Die Posada del Faro ist zudem ein guter Ausgangspunkt für Ausflüge – sei es in Badeorte wie Punta del Este oder La Paloma, zur Isla de Lobos mit ihrer Seelöwenkolonie oder auf den Cerro Catedral, mit 513 Metern der höchste Berg Uruguays!

Buchtipp: »Das Mädchen und der Feigenbaum« von Mario Benedetti

Une vue imprenable

Les paradis touristiques uruguayens se déploient à l'est de Montevideo et Punta del Este. Ici on voit des plages de sable blanc sur lesquelles viennent rouler les vagues du Rio de La Plata et de l'Atlantique, des petits villages dotés du nécessaire: magasins, restaurants et clubs. Quand la saison bat son plein, les touristes sont souvent très nombreux, mais il y a des exceptions: José Ignacio, à une trentaine de kilomètres de Punta del Este, est un endroit relativement paisible. On peut passer un été merveilleux à la Posada del Faro qui se dresse avec ses murs d'un blanc éclatant, ses voilages pare-soleil et ses parasols juste à trente mètres de l'océan – un panorama à couper le souffle. La piscine et le ciel (la plupart du temps) sont également voués au bleu, et l'intérieur de la maison réserve aussi des accents de cette couleur apaisante ici et là, sur les portes ou les tapis de sol.

Sinon des tons de crème et de bois naturel dominent dans les dix chambres. Chaque pièce est aménagée de manière individuelle mais toutes possèdent une terrasse protégée des regards et équipée de chaises longues ou de hamacs. Le soir tombé, lorsque le barbecue est allumé pour préparer l'« asado » typique et que les couverts sont disposés sur de longues tables, on a l'impression d'être chez des amis. En outre, la Posada del Faro est un bon point de départ pour les randonneurs, qu'ils désirent visiter les stations balnéaires de Punta del Este ou La Paloma, l'Isla de Lobos avec sa colonie de lions de mer ou le Cerro Catedral – le plus haut sommet d'Uruguay avec ses 513 mètres!

Livre à emporter: «La trêve» de Mario Benedetti

ANREISE	30 Kilometer nordöstlich von Punta del Este gelegen, direkt an der Atlantikküste
PREISE	$$
ZIMMER	10 individuell eingerichtete Doppelzimmer
KÜCHE	Kleines Grillrestaurant mit schöner Sicht aufs Meer
GESCHICHTE	Neue Adresse neben dem alten Leuchtturm anno 1877
X-FAKTOR	Wie eine private Villa abseits des Trubels

ACCÈS	Situé à 30 kilomètres au nord-est de Punta del Este, face à l'Atlantique
PRIX	$$
CHAMBRES	10 chambres doubles aménagées individuellement
RESTAURATION	Un petit restaurant de grillades avec belle vue sur la mer
HISTOIRE	Une nouvelle adresse à côté du vieux phare datant de 1877
LE « PETIT PLUS »	Comme une villa particulière, loin des bruits de la ville

Green spaces...
La Posada Estancia Agua Verde, Maldonado

La Posada Estancia
Agua Verde, Maldonado

Green spaces

Everyone should at least have seen Punta del Este, the cosmopolitan ocean resort on a peninsula between the River
Plate and the Atlantic, where the rich and famous (and of
course the wannabes) settle hotel bills as high as the cost
of a family saloon, dally the hours away on the beach or at
night-long parties in exclusive clubs, and are tracked each
and every summer by the press and TV reporters of Uruguay
and Argentina, anxious not to miss a moment. But spending
an entire vacation at South America's Monte Carlo is not for
everyone – nor, thank goodness, need it be. Just a mile or so
from Punta del Este there are magical country residences
awaiting guests who are out to discover the real Uruguay.
La Posada Estancia Agua Verde is one such, a horseshoe-
shaped farmhouse built in the late 18th century and now
converted into a hotel, set amidst an enchanted garden full
of chasing light and shadows. The suites and family apartment are furnished in a sturdy country style. Proprietress
Blanca Alvarez de Toledo breeds not only cattle and sheep
but also magnificent Arab horses – and a horseback ride
is the ideal way to get to know the gentle countryside all
around. (No need to worry about aching muscles when you
return – the hotel offers miraculous massages!). And it's
the perfect end to the day when the fragrances of genuine
country cooking prepared in the open on a charcoal burner
are wafted upon the evening air.

Book to pack: "Let the Wind Speak" by Juan Carlos Onetti

La Posada Estancia Agua Verde	
Camino Eguzquiza, km 7.5	
La Barra de Maldonado	
Punta del Este	
Uruguay	
Tel. (598) 42669941 and (598) 42670046	
E-mail: paz79@hotmail.com	
Website: www.estancias-uruguay.com	
www.great-escapes-hotels.com	

DIRECTIONS	7.5 km/5 miles from Punta del Este (airport transfer is organised)
RATES	$
ROOMS	5 suites (each with en suite bath), 1 apartment with 2 double rooms and bath
FOOD	Genuine Uruguayan home cooking
HISTORY	A late 18th-century country house converted to an appealing country inn
X-FACTOR	A farmstead vacation

Ganz im Grünen

Punta del Este muss man ein Mal gesehen haben – das
mondäne Seebad auf einer Halbinsel zwischen Río de la
Plata und Atlantik, wo die Schönen und Reichen (und sol-
che, die es gerne wären) Hotelrechnungen im Gegenwert
eines Mittelklassewagens begleichen, zwischen süßem
Nichtstun am Strand und nächtelangen Partys in Edelclubs
pendeln und Sommer für Sommer von Gazetten sowie Fern-
sehsendern aus ganz Uruguay und Argentinien auf Schritt
und Tritt beobachtet werden. Doch ein ganzer Urlaub im
Sylt Südamerikas ist nicht jedermanns Sache – und muss es
zum Glück auch gar nicht sein. Denn nur wenige Kilometer
von Punta del Este entfernt warten zauberhafte Landsitze
auf Gäste, die das ursprüngliche Uruguay kennenlernen
wollen – zum Beispiel La Posada Estancia Agua Verde. Das
U-förmige Farmhaus, das Ende des 18. Jahrhunderts gebaut
und inzwischen zum Hotel umfunktioniert wurde, liegt
inmitten eines verwunschenen Gartens voller Licht-und-
Schattenspiele und besitzt im robusten Countrystil einge-
richtete Suiten und ein Apartment für Familien. Besitzerin
Blanca Alvarez de Toledo züchtet neben Kühen und Schafen
auch prachtvolle Araberpferde, auf deren Rücken man die
sanfte Natur ringsum am besten erkundet (um eventuell
verspannte Muskeln muss sich niemand Sorgen machen,
denn im Hotel wirken Masseure Wunder!). Und der Tag
endet perfekt, wenn unter freiem Himmel und mit Hilfe
eines Holzkohleofens echte Landhausküche zubereitet wird.
**Buchtipp: »So traurig wie sie. Erzählungen« von Juan Carlos
Onetti**

Noyés dans la verdure

Punta del Este, située sur une presqu'île entre le Rio de La
Plata et l'Atlantique, est une station balnéaire réputée. Ici,
les gens les plus huppés, tous beaux et riches (ou qui vou-
draient l'être), paient des factures d'hôtel dont le montant
équivaut au prix d'une voiture de classe moyenne, passent
leurs journées à se dorer sur la plage et leurs nuits à faire
la fête dans des clubs privés et les casinos – et l'œil de la
presse et de la télévision uruguayenne et argentine à qui
rien n'échappe les observe été après été. On conviendra que
passer ses vacances ici n'est pas du goût de tout le monde.
Heureusement, à quelques kilomètres de Punta del Este, des
résidences enchanteresses attendent des hôtes qui s'intéressent à l'Uruguay authentique, celui des origines. La Posada
Estancia Agua Verde est l'une d'elles. Cette ferme en U,
construite à la fin du 18e siècle et transformée depuis en
hôtel, se dresse au milieu d'un jardin à la végétation exubérante où l'ombre joue avec la lumière. Elle possède des
suites et un appartement réservé aux familles, le tout aménagé dans un style rustique robuste. La propriétaire, Blanca
Alvarez de Toledo, élève des vaches et des moutons mais
aussi de magnifiques chevaux arabes. Ils sont à la disposi-
tion de ceux qui veulent explorer les paysages environnants,
et si les muscles des cavaliers sont endoloris par le manque
d'exercice, les masseurs de l'hôtel font des miracles. Et la
journée s'achève dans une douce quiétude quand la cuisine
traditionnelle du Rio de La Plata est préparée en plein air
sur un feu de charbon de bois.
**Livre à emporter : « Les bas-fonds du rêve » de Juan Carlos
Onetti**

ANREISE	7,5 Kilometer von Punta del Este entfernt (Transfer ab/an Flughafen wird organisiert)	ACCÈS	Situé à 7,5 kilomètres de Punta del Este (transfert organisé)
PREISE	$	PRIX	$
ZIMMER	5 Suiten (je mit privatem Bad), 1 Apartment mit 2 Doppelzimmern und einem Bad	CHAMBRES	5 suites (avec salle de bains), 1 appartement avec 2 chambres doubles et une salle de bains
KÜCHE	Echte Hausmannskost aus Uruguay	RESTAURATION	Authentique cuisine régionale uruguayenne
GESCHICHTE	Landhaus aus dem späten 18. Jahrhundert, zum hübschen Country Inn umgebaut	HISTOIRE	Villa de la fin du 18e siècle transformée en jolie auberge de campagne
X-FAKTOR	Ferien auf dem Bauernhof	LE « PETIT PLUS »	Des vacances à la ferme

Following nature's trail...
Yacutinga Lodge, Misiones

Following nature's trail

There are times when you long for the fantastic world of story-book adventures, that world of pursuits through the undergrowth of deep forests, with precarious suspended bridges spanning daunting chasms, leaves the size of surfboards meeting to roof the path with green, and toast roasted at the open campfire. The place to satisfy the craving is the Yacutinga Lodge, tucked away in the jungle borderlands between Argentina and Brazil. The buildings, made of local stone and thick wooden planks, mantled softly in green and appointed with organically-shaped furniture and with fabrics in muted hues, were designed to harmonise with the enchanting natural setting. Yacutinga is an all-round environmental venture, and offers ecotourism complete with every comfort – guests live not just *in* but *with* nature. Around the Lodge is a 570-hectare private reserve, which in turn is part of a 270,000-hectare conservation area – in contrast to much of the region, no forest clearing is permitted here. More than 2,000 plant species and some 400 species of animals benefit from this. To walk through the forest is to feel you're in some vast Jungle Book, with butterflies, snakes, monkeys, and birds waiting to be discovered. Professional guides accompany all excursions, on foot or by boat, or indeed at night, when the sounds and smells are muted and lend the forest a very special magic. It's worth planning at least three days at the Lodge, but most guests stay much longer anyway – because Yacutinga does have this in common with the adventure story realm: once you're there, you'll never want to leave.

Book to pack: "Concerning the Angels" by Rafael Alberti

Yacutinga Lodge	
Lote 7a	
3371 Almte, Brown	
Misiones	
Argentina	
Tel. (54) 937 51664242	
E-mail: yacutinga@yacutinga.net	
Website: www.yacutinga.com	
www.great-escapes-hotels.com	

DIRECTIONS	Situated in the far northeast of Argentina, 60 km/38 miles from Iguazú. Transfer from Puesto Tigre/Iguazú Falls is organised, by road and boat
RATES	$$
ROOMS	6 double rooms, 14 three-bed rooms
FOOD	Fresh produce grown in the Lodge's own kitchen gardens. Open-air barbecues
HISTORY	Conceived as a dream destination for modern eco-tourists
X-FACTOR	A green thought in a green shade

Der Natur auf der Spur

Manchmal wünscht man sich ja auf diese fantastischen Abenteuerspielplätze zurück: Wo man im tiefsten Wald durchs Gebüsch pirschte und auf Hängebrücken gefährlich aussehende Schluchten überquerte, wo Blätter so groß wie Surfbretter grüne Dächer über den Wegen bildeten und wo am offenen Feuer Stockbrot geröstet werden konnte. Diese Sehnsucht kann gestillt werden – mit einer Reise zur Yacutinga Lodge, die sich im Dschungel an der Grenze zwischen Argentinien und Brasilien versteckt. In Harmonie mit der verwunschenen Natur wurden hier Häuser aus einheimischem Stein und dicken Holzplanken gebaut, jedes von Grün umhüllt wie von einem weichen Mantel und mit organisch geformten Möbeln sowie Stoffen in weichen Tönen ausgestattet. Yacutinga ist ein umfassendes Umweltprojekt und verspricht komfortablen Ökotourismus – es lässt seine Gäste nicht nur in der Natur, sondern mit der Natur leben. Rings um die Lodge dehnt sich ein 570 Hektar großes Privatreservat aus, das wiederum Teil eines 270.000 Hektar großen Schutzgebietes ist – hier darf im Gegensatz zu weiten Teilen der Region nicht gerodet werden. Mehr als 2.000 verschiedene Pflanzen- und rund 400 Tierarten profitieren davon; wer durch den Wald wandert, fühlt sich wie in einem überdimensionalen Dschungelbuch, entdeckt Schmetterlinge, Schlangen, Affen und Vögel. Professionelle Führer begleiten jede Exkursion – sei es zu Fuß, per Boot oder sogar während der Nacht, wenn die Geräusche und Gerüche weicher werden und dem Wald einen ganz besonderen Zauber verleihen. Mindestens drei Tage sollte man sich für die Lodge Zeit nehmen, doch die meisten Gäste bleiben ohnehin viel länger – denn auch darin ähneln sich ein Abenteuerspielplatz und Yacutinga: Ist man einmal dort, will man nie wieder weg.

Buchtipp: »Die Engel« von Rafael Alberti

Vacances vertes

Parfois on se surprend à avoir la nostalgie de ces fantastiques terrains de jeux d'aventure : on s'en allait courageusement à la chasse dans les taillis épais, on traversait des gorges dangereuses sur des ponts suspendus ; d'immenses feuilles vertes recouvraient les sentiers et on pouvait faire griller du pain sec sur des feux de camp. On peut retrouver tout cela au Yacutinga Lodge qui se dissimule dans la jungle à la frontière argentino-brésilienne.

Les quatre habitations construites ici en harmonie avec la nature avec la pierre locale et des planches épaisses, sont habillées de verdure et abritent des meubles aux formes organiques et des étoffes aux teintes pastelles. Yacutinga, projet écologique de vaste envergure, offre un refuge confortable aux adeptes du tourisme vert – les hôtes ne vivent pas seulement dans la nature, ils vivent avec la nature. Tout autour du Lodge se déploie une réserve naturelle privée de 570 hectares, elle-même faisant partie du « corridor vert » d'Iguazú, un secteur de 270.000 hectares dans lequel il est interdit de déboiser, contrairement à ce qui se passe dans de vastes zones de la région.

Plus de 2.000 espèces végétales et environ 400 espèces animales vivent ici : celui qui se balade en forêt découvre des papillons, des serpents, des singes et des oiseaux. Des guides naturalistes professionnels accompagnent toutes les excursions, qu'elles se fassent à pied, en bateau, ou la nuit quand les animaux sont actifs, quand les bruits et les odeurs se font plus lourds et donnent à la forêt un charme particulier. Il est recommandé de rester au moins trois jours au Lodge, mais la plupart des hôtes y séjournent beaucoup plus longtemps. C'est aussi le point commun entre Yacutinga et le terrain de jeux d'aventure – une fois que l'on y a pris goût, on ne veut plus le quitter.

Livre à emporter : « Marin à terre » de Rafael Alberti

ANREISE	Im äußersten Nordosten Argentiniens gelegen, 60 Kilometer von Iguazú entfernt. Transfer ab Puesto Tigre/Iguazú Wasserfälle per Auto und Boot wird organisiert
PREISE	$$
ZIMMER	6 Doppelzimmer, 14 Dreibettzimmer
KÜCHE	Frisches aus eigenem Anbau, Barbecues unter freiem Himmel
GESCHICHTE	Als Traumziel für moderne Ökotouristen konzipiert
X-FAKTOR	Alles im grünen Bereich

ACCÈS	Situé à l'extrême nord-est de l'Argentine, à 60 kilomètres d'Iguazú. Transfert en voiture et en bateau organisé à partir de Puesto Tigre/Chutes d'Iguazú
PRIX	$$
CHAMBRES	6 chambres doubles, 14 chambres à trois lits
RESTAURATION	Avec des produits frais cultivés sur place (le Lodge a son propre potager). Barbecues en plein air
HISTOIRE	Pour les touristes respectueux de l'environnement
LE « PETIT PLUS »	Des vacances vertes

A jungle lodge...
Posada La Bonita, Misiones

Posada La Bonita, Misiones

A jungle lodge

This jungle is more like an enchanted forest in a fairy tale. The green of the twined plants is so rich you almost think it's dripping from the leaves. A faint veil seems always to be drifting upon the air, and a tremendous waterfall is tumbling into the depths. Never has it been so easy to achieve a state resembling that of meditation – the Posada La Bonita grants the soul the very best, from the very first moment. A jungle lodge in the extreme northeastern of Argentina, it is entirely one with its natural setting. The rooms are done in an abundance of wood and hand-woven fabrics, and with greenery visible from every room and veranda you won't miss the high-tech environment of the world you've left behind for a single second. The perfect day in La Bonita begins with the dawn chorus and breakfast in the open, and then it's time to explore the labyrinthine river system and forests in a kayak or hand-carved canoe, or get to know the country on horseback. After a candlelight dinner with lounge music in the background you can idle for a while in a hammock before turning in – no need to worry about mosquitoes, since they rarely make an appearance at this altitude. At this hour, the soothing splash of the waterfall is better than any sleeping pill. And if you find the sheer fascination of water is getting to you, try visiting the nearby Saltos del Moconá, where the Uruguay River races down three kilometres (1.8 miles) of breathtaking cascades.

Book to pack: "What the Night Tells the Day"
by Hector Bianciotti

Posada La Bonita	**DIRECTIONS** Situated 300 km/188 miles southeast of Iguazú airport. The transfer is organised
Moconá, El Soberbio	**RATES** $
Misiones	**ROOMS** 6 double rooms
Argentina	**FOOD** Regional and Italian cuisine, with a substantial range of vegetarian fare
Tel. (54) 375515680380 and (54) 111544908386	
E-mail: posadalabonita@hotmail.com	**HISTORY** Opened in March 1999
Website: www.posadalabonita.com.ar	**X-FACTOR** The full glorious spectacle of nature
www.great-escapes-hotels.com	

Dschungellodge

Dieser Urwald ist ein Märchenwald: Die ineinander ver-
schlungenen Pflanzen sind so sattgrün, dass man glaubt, die
Farbe von den Blättern tropfen zu sehen, in der Luft scheint
immer ein leichter Schleier zu schweben, und ein mächtiger
Wasserfall stürzt in die Tiefe. Nie war es so einfach, sich in
einen meditationsähnlichen Zustand zu versetzen – wer in
die Posada La Bonita zieht, gönnt seiner Seele vom ersten
Moment an nur das Beste. Die Dschungellodge im äußers-
ten Nordosten Argentiniens ist mit der Natur verwachsen,
hier wohnt man in mit viel Holz und handgewebten Stoffen
ausgestatteten Zimmern, blickt von jedem Raum und jeder
Veranda aus ins Grüne und vermisst die High-Tech-Errun-
genschaften der restlichen Welt keine Sekunde lang. Der
perfekte Tag in La Bonita beginnt mit einem Konzert der
Vögel und einem Frühstück im Freien, anschließend spürt
man vom Kajak oder handgeschnitzten Kanu aus die
Geheimnisse der Flusslabyrinthe und des Waldes auf oder
entdeckt die Umgebung per Pferd. Nach einem Abendessen
bei Kerzenschein und mit Loungemusik im Hintergrund
schaukelt man in der Hängematte der Nacht entgegen und
muss sich dabei nicht vor Mückenstichen fürchten – dank
der Höhenlage kommen die angriffslustigen Insekten hier
so gut wie gar nicht vor. Das Plätschern des Wasserfalls
wirkt zu später Stunde dann besser als jede Baldriantablette
– wen während des Urlaubs die Faszination des nassen Ele-
ments nicht mehr loslässt, der sollte auch zu den nahen
Saltos del Moconá fahren, wo der Fluss Uruguay auf einer
Länge von drei Kilometern eine rauschende Kaskade bildet.
Buchtipp: »Wie die Spur des Vogels in der Luft«
von Hector Bianciotti

Lodge de la jungle

Cette forêt semble sortie tout droit d'un conte de fées : les
plantes qui s'entrelacent sont d'un vert si intense que l'on
croit voir la couleur goutter de leurs feuilles, un voile léger
de condensation flotte dans l'air et une imposante cascade se
jette dans les profondeurs. Jamais il n'a été aussi facile qu'ici
de se retrouver dans un état proche de la méditation – celui
qui réside à la Posada La Bonita peut choyer son âme dès le
premier moment. Situé à l'extrême nord-est de l'Argentine,
ce lodge est intimement lié à la nature environnante. Le bois
et les étoffes tissées à la main abondent dans les chambres
qui offrent toutes, ainsi que les vérandas, une vue sur la
verdure. Ici, on ne regrette pas une seconde les progrès tech-
nologiques du reste du monde. À La Bonita, la journée commence avec le chant des oiseaux au réveil et un petit-déjeuner en plein air. Ensuite, on part en kayak ou dans un canoë
gravé à la main, à la découverte des mystères du fleuve et de
la forêt ou bien on fait une randonnée à cheval. Après un
dîner aux chandelles avec une musique douce en fond sono-
re, on peut savourer la tombée de la nuit dans un hamac.
Nulle crainte à avoir des moustiques, il n'y en a pratiquement pas à cette altitude. Le murmure au loin de la cascade
fait plus d'effet que n'importe quelle pilule pour dormir. Et
si pendant ces vacances, la fascination de l'eau ne vous quit-
te plus, allez donc visiter les chutes Saltos del Moconá, là où
le fleuve Uruguay forme sur trois kilomètres une cascade
impressionnante.
Livre à emporter : « Comme la trace de l'oiseau dans l'air »
de Hector Bianciotti

ANREISE	300 Kilometer südöstlich des Flughafens Iguazú gelegen. Transfer wird organisiert
PREISE	$
ZIMMER	6 Doppelzimmer
KÜCHE	Regionale und italienische Menüs, großes Angebot für Vegetarier
GESCHICHTE	Im März 1999 eröffnet
X-FAKTOR	Ein Naturschauspiel

ACCÈS	Situé à 300 kilomètres au sud-est de l'aéroport d'Iguazú. Le transfert est organisé
PRIX	$
CHAMBRES	6 chambres doubles
RESTAURATION	Menus régionaux et italiens. Grand choix de plats végétariens
HISTOIRE	Ouvert en mars 1999
LE « PETIT PLUS »	Un spectacle de la nature

Homage to fine wine...
Bodega El Esteco de Cafayate, Salta

Homage to fine wine

It's almost like being in the old heart of a Spanish town. Through the imposing arched gateways you come upon whitewashed buildings with rounded arches, bell towers and patios, with geraniums and roses to fill the scene with colour and fragrance. And that first impression is absolutely right: the colonial-inspired architecture of the Bodega El Esteco de Cafayate was modelled on the Barrio de la Santa Cruz, the historic centre of Seville. Still, the surroundings quickly remind you that you're in South America. All around the estate are vineyards, stretching as far as the horizon, it seems, or at least to the Andean Cordilleras. The grapes that grow in the Valles Calchaquíes are first class, thanks to the 340 days of sunshine per annum, the cool nights, and an ideal high-lying location some 1,700 metres (about 5,300 feet) above sea level – and the local wine-growers export their vintages all over the world. The Bodega El Esteco de Cafayate (hitherto also known to aficionados as the Bodega La Rosa) was established in 1892 by two brothers, David and Salvador Michel, who haled from Catalonia. Currently it is being re-structured as a kind of boutique winery: only choice wines will be produced in the future, bearing names such as "Don David" or "Altimus". This exclusivity is the hallmark of the country hotel as well. Offering the authentic experience of the vintner's way of life on a private farmhouse, without losing out on any of the comforts and amenities of a modern hotel. The leisure programme includes vineyard tours, photo expeditions, riding, trekking, and fishing trips. Regardless of which programme you opt for, the finest hours may well be those that begin at sunset, when real country cooking is served in the inviting dining rooms – with the estate's own fine wines.

Book to pack: "Imagining Argentina" by Lawrence Thornton

Bodega El Esteco de Cafayate
Ruta Nacional 40 y Ruta Nacional 68
4427 Cafayate
Salta
Argentina
Tel. (54) 3868422229
Fax (54) 3868421753
E-mail: jradavero@micheltorino.com.ar
Website: www.micheltorino.com.ar
www.great-escapes-hotels.com

DIRECTIONS	Situated 120 km/75 miles (two and a half hours by road) south of Salta
RATES	$$$
ROOMS	30 double rooms
FOOD	Argentine country food, with first-class wines
HISTORY	A 19th-century winery with hotel & spa added in 2005
X-FACTOR	In vino veritas

Dem Wein gewidmet

Man könnte meinen, in einer spanischen Altstadt zu sein:
Hinter mächtigen Torbögen liegen weiß getünchte Gebäude
mit Rundbögen, Glockentürmen und Patios, in denen Gera-
nien oder Rosen für süßen Duft und Farbe sorgen. Und
wirklich ist die kolonial angehauchte Architektur der Bodega
El Esteco de Cafayate dem Barrio de la Santa Cruz, dem historischen Zentrum Sevillas, nachempfunden – doch das
Umland holt einen schnell nach Südamerika zurück. Rings
um das Anwesen dehnt sich ein Weinanbaugebiet aus, das
bis zum Horizont oder zumindest bis zur Andenkordillere
im Hintergrund zu reichen scheint. Mehr als 340 Sonnentage, kühle Nächte und eine ideale Höhenlage von 1.700
Metern lassen in den Valles Calchaquíes erstklassige Trau-
ben reifen – hier ansässige Winzer exportieren ihre Tropfen
in alle Welt. Die Bodega El Esteco de Cafayate (Insidern war
sie bislang auch als Bodega La Rosa bekannt) wurde 1892
von den ursprünglich katalanischen Brüdern David und Salvador Michel gegründet und wird derzeit zu einer Art »Bou-
tique-Winery« umstrukturiert: Nur noch Spitzenweine mit
klingenden Namen wie »Don David« oder »Altimus« sollen
künftig produziert werden. Ebenso exklusiv geht es auch im
angeschlossenen Landhotel zu. Hier soll man das Winzerle-
ben wie in einem privaten Farmhaus erleben, ohne auf die
Annehmlichkeiten eines modernen Hotels verzichten zu
müssen. Auf dem Entspannungsprogramm stehen Touren
durch die Wineyards, Fotosafaris, Ausritte, Trekkings und
Angelausflüge. Doch ganz egal, für welches Programm man
sich entscheidet: Die vielleicht schönsten Stunden beginnen
bei Sonnenuntergang, wenn in den gemütlichen Gutsräumen
echte Landhausküche serviert wird – und dazu feine Weine
aus eigenem Anbau im Glas glänzen.

Buchtipp: »Wiedersehen in Argentinien« von Hubert Landes

Le goût du vin

On se croirait dans une vieille cité espagnole : derrière de
vastes portails s'élèvent des bâtiments blancs dotés d'arches
en plein cintre, de clochers et de patios dans lesquels des
géraniums ou des roses apportent des accents de couleur et
des odeurs suaves. L'architecture aux accents coloniaux de la
Bodega El Esteco de Cafayate est réellement inspirée de celle
du Barrio de la Santa Cruz, le cœur historique de Séville.
Mais l'illusion se dissipe rapidement car, autour de la propriété, les vignobles semblent se déployer jusqu'à la cordillère des Andes. Avec plus de 340 journées d'ensoleillement,
des nuits fraîches et une altitude de près de 1700 mètres au-
dessus du niveau de la mer, les Valles Calchaquies voient
mûrir des raisins de premier choix – les viticulteurs de la
région exportent leurs crus dans le monde entier.
La Bodega El Esteco de Cafayate (jusqu'ici Bodega La Rosa
pour les initiés), fondée en 1892 par les frères d'origine cata-
lane David et Salvador Michel, est en cours de restructura-
tion et ne produira bientôt plus que des vins exceptionnels
au doux nom de « Don David » ou « Altimus ». L'hôtel
annexe subit la même métamorphose luxueuse. Les hôtes
doivent vivre ici comme à la ferme sans renoncer aux com-
modités d'un hôtel moderne.
Le programme-détente prévoit des randonnées à travers la
région viticole, des safaris photo, du trekking et des excursions de pêche. Mais les heures les plus douces seront sans
doute celles que l'on passe après le coucher du soleil quand
la bonne cuisine rustique est servie dans les salles
accueillantes – sans oublier les vins délectables produits
sur le terroir.

Livre à emporter : « La trame céleste » de Adolfo Bioy Casares

ANREISE	120 Kilometer (zweieinhalb Fahrtstunden) südlich von Salta gelegen
PREISE	$$$
ZIMMER	30 Doppelzimmer
KÜCHE	Argentinische Landhausküche, erstklassige Weine
GESCHICHTE	Ein Weingut aus dem 19. Jahrhundert, seit 2005 mit Hotel & Spa
X-FAKTOR	In vino veritas

ACCÈS	Situé à 20 kilomètres (deux heures et demie de voiture) au sud de Salta
PRIX	$$$
CHAMBRES	30 chambres doubles
RESTAURATION	Cuisine de pays, vins de premier choix
HISTOIRE	Un vignoble du 19e siècle, inclu hôtel et spa depuis 2005
LE « PETIT PLUS »	In vino veritas

A remote world by the water

Pirá Lodge, Corrientes Province

A remote world by the water

It's called the tiger of the rivers – *salminus maxillosus*, with its shimmering yellow scales, razor-sharp teeth, and power-ful fins, which enable it to glide through the water at an extraordinary speed. The best place to go in pursuit of this salmon-like fish is the swamplands of Iberá, a region of crys-tal-clear rivers and shallow inlets, virtually untouched by humankind and almost twice the size of Florida's Ever-glades. For anglers and fly fishermen, this part of northern Argentina is still an insider's tip – as is the Pirá Lodge, in Corrientes Province. It is not remotely what you would nor-mally expect a fishermen's hotel to be: there are no fusty odours, no rods to trip over, and the accommodation doesn't consist of four-bed dorms. Here, a maximum of ten guests reside comfortably in five well-appointed double rooms. They're light and airy, the furniture is hand-crafted, and a bath with a view is included in the price. The Pirá Lodge is country style of a sophisticated order, complete with a 20-metre (66 feet) pool and a barbecue restaurant, well-trai-ned staff, and an angling store on the hotel premises. The season runs from September to April; but the Pirá is open outside this period too, and affords visitors at all times the opportunity to explore the countryside on horseback or in a kayak – or simply to enjoy the sun.

Book to pack: "The House of Bernarda Alba" by Federico Garcia Lorca

Pirá Lodge c/o Nervous Waters Av. Figueroa Alcorta 3351, 2nd floor, 228 office C1425CKM Buenos Aires Tel. (54) 1148011008 E-mail: santiago@nervouswaters.com Website: www.piralodge.com www.great-escapes-hotels.com	**DIRECTIONS** Situated 640 km/400 miles north of Buenos Aires. The flight to Resistencia or Corrientes costs US$ 350 per per-son. The transfer to the Lodge takes about four hours and is organised for guests **RATES** $$ **ROOMS** 5 double rooms (each with en suite bath) **FOOD** Very good Argentine home cooking **HISTORY** One of the country's most recently established fishing lodges, small and select **X-FACTOR** An active vacation in first-class fishing country

Ferne Welt am Wasser

Er gilt als der »Tiger der Flüsse« – der *Salminus Maxillosus*
mit seinen gelb schimmernden Schuppen, seinen scharfen
Zähnen und seinen starken Flossen, die ihn im Rekordtem-
po durchs Wasser gleiten lassen. Wer auf die Jagd nach diesem lachsähnlichen Fisch gehen möchte, tut dies am besten
in den Sümpfen von Iberá, einem Marschland aus kristallklaren Flüssen und seichten Buchten, fast unberührt und
fast zweieinhalbmal so groß wie die Everglades in Florida.
Unter Sport- und Fliegenfischern gilt diese Region im Norden Argentiniens noch als Geheimtipp – genau so wie die
Pirá Lodge, die in der Provinz Corrientes ihre Pforten geöffnet hat. Sie ist weit entfernt von allem, was man sich im All-
gemeinen unter einem Hotel für Angler vorstellt: Hier liegt
kein modriger Geruch in der Luft, man stolpert nicht ständig über Ruten und schläft auch nicht in Vierbettzimmern –
hier logieren maximal zehn Gäste in fünf komfortablen
Doppelzimmern; viel Licht, handgefertigte Möbel und eine
Badewanne mit Aussicht inbegriffen. Ganz im Sinne des
gehobenen Countrystils gehören auch ein 20-Meter-Pool
und ein Grillrestaurant zur Lodge, und die fischenden
Gäste freuen sich über gut ausgebildetes Personal und einen
hoteleigenen Anglershop. Saison ist hier von September bis
April; doch Pirá hat auch außerhalb dieser Monate geöffnet
und empfängt dann vor allem Besucher, die die umliegende
Natur hoch zu Pferd oder im Kajak erkunden – oder einfach
nur die Sonne genießen.

Buchtipp: »Bernarda Albas Haus« von Federico Garcia Lorca

Ici l'on pêche

Avec ses écailles aux reflets jaunes, ses dents acérées et ses
nageoires puissantes qui lui permettent de glisser dans
l'eau à toute allure, le dorado *Salminus Maxillosus* est le
« tigre del rio ». Les amateurs peuvent pêcher ce poisson qui
ressemble au saumon dans les marais d'Iberá, un delta de
rivières cristallines et de baies peu profondes, pratiquement
vierges et deux fois et demie plus vaste que les Everglades
de Floride. Cette région du nord de l'Argentine n'est encore
connue que de quelques clubs de pêche et de pêcheurs à la
mouche – et c'est aussi le cas du Pirá Lodge qui a ouvert
ses portes dans la province de Corrientes.
Il ne ressemble pas à l'hôtel pour pêcheurs tels qu'on
l'imagine en général : ici pas d'odeur de vase, pas de
cannes à pêche où l'on se prend sans cesse les pieds et pas
de chambres à quatre lits. L'endroit peut loger dix personnes
dans cinq chambres doubles confortables. La lumière abondante, des meubles faits à la main et une baignoire avec vue
sont compris dans la location. Tout à fait dans l'esprit du
style Country élégant, une piscine de 20 mètres de long et
un restaurant à grillades font également partie du Lodge, et
les hôtes sont satisfaits du personnel aimable et compétent
et de la boutique offrant des articles de pêche qui appartient
à l'hôtel.
La saison de pêche débute au mois de septembre et s'achève
en avril, mais Pirá est ouvert toute l'année et accueille surtout des visiteurs qui veulent explorer la nature environnante à cheval ou en kayak, ou simplement profiter du soleil.

**Livre à emporter : « La maison de Bernarda Alba » de Federico
Garcia Lorca**

ANREISE	640 Kilometer nördlich von Buenos Aires gelegen. Flug nach Resistencia oder Corrientes US$ 350 pro Person. Rund vierstündige Weiterfahrt zur Lodge wird organisiert
PREISE	$$
ZIMMER	5 Doppelzimmer. Mit je eigenem Bad
KÜCHE	Sehr gute argentinische Hausmannskost
GESCHICHTE	Eine der jüngsten Fishing-Lodges des Landes, klein und fein
X-FAKTOR	Aktivurlaub in einem erstklassigen Anglerrevier

ACCÈS	Situé à 640 kilomètres au nord de Buenos Aires. Vols à destination de Resistencia ou Corrientes US$ 350 par personne. Le trajet de quatre heures vers le Lodge est organisé
PRIX	$$
CHAMBRES	5 chambres doubles (avec salle de bains)
RESTAURATION	Excellente cuisine argentine
HISTOIRE	Un des plus récents Fishing-Lodges du pays
LE « PETIT PLUS »	Des vacances actives dans une zone de pêche de premier choix

Roaming further afield...

Dos Lunas, Province Córdoba

Roaming further afield

It was at Mount Colchequin that the indigenous Comechingones suffered their worst moment. Faced on this rocky terrain with defeat at the hands of the Spanish, they leapt from the peak to their deaths, preferring to die with pride rather than on Spanish pikes. Happily, this onetime battleground is now a peaceful place. To gaze across the green and gently undulating country of Ongamira, where weather-rounded rocks repose like slumbering creatures of fantasy with russet-brown backs, is to behold a soft and tranquil landscape. And it is here that we find the Dos Lunas country hotel, in the heart of 3,000 hectares of what seems utterly unspoilt nature. For new arrivals, the best way to acclimatise to the vast and peaceful spaces of Córdoba province is to relax by the pool in the garden; but no later than day two you should be out and about, exploring the region. Take a long walk through the forests and hills, for instance, forever moving on from one breathtaking lookout point to the next. Or if you want to roam further afield, Dos Lunas offers horse riding – from short canters, to excursions into the mountains, to trekking expeditions lasting days. If you opt for the long version, you'll spend your nights camping in the open, listening to the guides' tales and guitar playing by the campfire. If you're a little weary on your return, and your muscles are aching, Dos Lunas has all the creature comfort you need, and hot baths to relax in. The establishment is also celebrated for its country cooking – from breakfast with homebaked break and honey from the region to barbecues by the pool, this is the taste of Argentina!

Book to pack: "Don Segundo Sombra" by Ricardo Güiraldes

Dos Lunas	
Alto Ongamira, Todos los Santos, Ischillin	
Province Córdoba	
Argentina	
Tel. (54) 1150323410 and (54) 91162195390	
E-mail: doslunas@doslunas.com.ar	
Website: www.doslunas.com.ar	
www.great-escapes-hotels.com	

DIRECTIONS	Situated 120 km/75 miles north of Córdoba (domestic flights from Buenos Aires), 90 minutes by road. The transfer costs US$ 90
RATES	$
ROOMS	8 double rooms
FOOD	Good, substantial fare, using regional produce
HISTORY	A modern country hotel on historic ground
X-FACTOR	Nature pure and simple – as far as the eye can see

Ein weites Feld

Am Berg Colchequin musste der Stamm der Comechingones einst seine größte Niederlage hinnehmen: Die Indianer drohten auf dem felsigen Gelände den Kampf gegen die Spanier zu verlieren und stürzten sich vom Gipfel in den Tod, um zumindest mit Stolz zu sterben und nicht durch spanische Speere. Der einstige Kampfplatz präsentiert sich heute zum Glück friedvoll: Wer über das leicht gewellte und grüne Land von Ongamira blickt, in dem rund geschliffene Felsen wie schlafende Fantasiewesen mit rotbraunen Rücken liegen, sieht eine sanfte und stille Landschaft. Hier steht auch das Landhotel Dos Lunas – inmitten von 3.000 Hektar wie unberührt wirkender Natur. Neuankömmlinge gewöhnen sich am besten am runden Pool im Garten an die Ruhe und Weitläufigkeit der Provinz Córdoba; doch spätestens am zweiten Tag sollte man die Region aktiv erkunden. Zum Beispiel bei einem langen Spaziergang durch die Wälder und Hügel und immer auf der Suche nach einem Aussichtspunkt, der noch schöner als der vorhergehende ist. Wen es noch weiter hinaus zieht, für den bietet Dos Lunas Touren hoch zu Ross an – von kurzen Ausritten über Ausflüge in die Berge bis hin zu tagelangen Trekkings ist alles möglich. Wer sich für die Maxiversion entscheidet, campiert nachts im Freien, lauscht den Legenden der Guides und ihrem Gitarrenspiel am Lagerfeuer. Vielleicht schmerzen die Muskeln anschließend ein wenig und vielleicht kommt man ein bisschen müde zurück; doch Dos Lunas sorgt mit gemütlichem Komfort und heißen Bädern für Entspannung. Berühmt ist das Haus auch für seine Landhausküche – vom Frühstück mit selbst gebackenem Brot und regionalem Honig bis hin zum Barbecue am Pool: So schmeckt Argentinien!

Buchtipp: »Das Buch vom Gaucho Sombra« von Ricardo Güiraldes

Les grands espaces

C'est sur la montagne de Colchequin que la tribu des Comechingones a subi l'une de ses plus terribles défaites. Alors qu'ils étaient sur le point d'être vaincus par les Espagnols, les Indiens préférèrent se jeter dans le vide plutôt que de se rendre. Ils voulaient mourir dans la dignité et non pas par les lances de leurs ennemis. L'ancien champ de bataille a retrouvé aujourd'hui un aspect serein. Légèrement vallonné, le territoire d'Ongamira se distingue par sa douceur et sa tranquillité, les rochers aux formes arrondies ressemblent à des êtres fabuleux assoupis dont on ne verrait que le dos rougeâtre. C'est ici qu'est situé également l'hôtel de campagne Dos Lunas – au milieu d'une nature de 3000 hectares qui semble être restée intacte. Les nouveaux venus s'acclimateront au calme et à l'immensité de la province de Córdoba en se prélassant près de la piscine ronde dans le jardin. Mais après une journée de repos, nous leur recommandons de partir à la découverte de la région en faisant, par exemple, une longue promenade à travers les forêts et les collines, à la recherche des points de vue, tous plus beaux les uns que les autres. Pour celui qui désire s'aventurer plus loin, Dos Lunas propose des randonnées à cheval : petites virées dans les montagnes ou excursions de plusieurs jours, tout est possible. Si vous vous décidez pour la dernière solution, vous dormirez à la belle étoile, vous écouterez, allongé près du feu de camp, vos guides jouer de la guitare et vous conter les légendes du pays. Peut-être reviendrez-vous un peu fatigué et courbatu à Dos Lunas, mais avec son confort et ses bains chauds, l'hôtel vous invitera à la détente. Sa célèbre cuisine campagnarde vous redonnera aussi le punch nécessaire : petit déjeuner avec pain cuit maison et miel de la région, barbecue au bord de la piscine, c'est tout le goût de l'Argentine !

Livre à emporter : « Don Segundo Sombra » de Ricardo Güiraldes

ANREISE	120 Kilometer nördlich von Córdoba gelegen (dorthin Inlandsflüge ab Buenos Aires), Fahrtzeit 90 Minuten. Der Transfer kostet US$ 90
PREISE	$
ZIMMER	8 Doppelzimmer
KÜCHE	Gut, kräftig und mit regionalen Produkten
GESCHICHTE	Modernes Landhotel auf geschichtsträchtigem Boden
X-FAKTOR	Natur pur – bis zum Horizont

ACCÈS	Situé à 120 kilomètres au nord de Córdoba (vols intérieurs depuis Buenos Aires), trajet 90 minutes. Le transfert coûte US$ 90
PRIX	$
CHAMBRES	8 chambres doubles
RESTAURATION	Bonne cuisine rustique avec des produits régionaux
HISTOIRE	Hôtel de campagne sur un territoire chargé d'histoire
LE « PETIT PLUS »	De la nature à perte de vue

Staying with the President...

Estancia La Paz, Province Córdoba

Estancia La Paz, Province Córdoba

Staying with the President

"My political commitment never prevented me from maintaining a habit I was fond of. Every summer I spent at least two months in La Paz". The words are those of Julio Argentino Roca, President of Argentina from 1880 to 1886 and from 1898 to 1904 and a member of the "Generación del 80", a political/intellectual group that stood for immigration, economic growth, and a strong middle class. The gentlemen of the group debated their plans for reform not only in the capital, Buenos Aires, but also 110 kilometres (70 miles) away at Ascochinga, in the President's country house. For Julio Argentino Roca, La Paz was at once a private summer residence and a political meeting place – and the grand state style of that stance can still be sensed at the Estancia today. You reside in yellow-painted, lovingly restored buildings in the style of the colonial era or the Italian Renaissance, stroll in the vast and tranquil park laid out by French landscape architect Charles Thays, or take a dip in the pool, which at Roca's request was the first in the entire province to be of Olympic size. This is Argentine country life *de luxe* – naturally La Paz has two polo pitches as well, where national events take place, not to mention a first-rate 18-hole golf course the grass on which looks so manicured that you picture the head greenkeeper personally trimming each blade of grass with nail-clippers. And when it's time to adjourn to the nineteenth hole, if you're in luck the restaurant is serving the typical "cocina criolla" or there's a barbecue. Small wonder the master of the house used to feel a two-month summer break at La Paz was the absolute minimum.
Book to pack: "The Aleph" by Jorge Luis Borges

Estancia La Paz	
Ruta E66, km 14, Asochinga	
Province Córdoba	
Argentina	
Tel. and fax (54) 3525 492073	
E-mail: info@estancialapaz.com	
Website: www.estancialapaz.com	
www.great-escapes-hotels.com	

DIRECTIONS	Situated 50 km/30 miles northeast of Córdoba airport (domestic flights from Buenos Aires)
RATES	$
ROOMS	2 three-bed rooms, 19 double rooms, 1 Presidential Suite
FOOD	Regional specialities (cocina criolla) and typical Argentine barbecue (asado)
HISTORY	What was once the President's country residence is now a luxurious country hotel
X-FACTOR	A summer break such as statesmen prefer

Zu Gast beim Präsidenten

»Mein politisches Engagement hat mich niemals von einer lieb gewonnenen Routine abgehalten: Ich verbrachte jeden Sommer mindestens zwei Monate in La Paz« – diese Zeilen stammen aus der Feder von Julio Argentino Roca, Argentiniens Präsident von 1880 bis 1886 sowie 1898 bis 1904 und Mitglied der politisch-intellektuellen Gruppe »Generación del 80«, die auf Einwanderung, Wirtschaftswachstum und einen starken Mittelstand setzte. Ihre Reformpläne diskutierten die Herren nicht nur in der Hauptstadt Buenos Aires, sondern auch im 110 Kilometer entfernten Ascochinga, im Landhaus des Präsidenten. La Paz war für Julio Argentino Roca privater Sommersitz und politischer Treffpunkt zugleich – und dieses staatstragende Flair verströmt die Estancia noch heute. Hier residiert man in gelb gestrichenen und liebevoll restaurierten Gebäuden im Stil der Kolonialzeit und der italienischen Renaissance, flaniert durch den weitläufigen und friedlichen Park, der die Handschrift des französischen Landschaftsarchitekten Charles Thays trägt, oder taucht im Pool unter, der auf Rocas Wunsch hin der erste mit olympischen Ausmaßen in der gesamten Provinz war. Es ist argentinisches Landleben de luxe – denn natürlich dürfen auf La Paz auch zwei Polo-Felder nicht fehlen, auf denen nationale Turniere ausgetragen werden, sowie ein anspruchsvoller 18-Loch-Golfplatz, dessen Rasen so gepflegt wirkt, als stutzte der Chef-Greenkeeper jeden einzelnen Grashalm persönlich mit der Nagelschere. Wer nach einer guten Runde dann noch das Glück hat, im Restaurant typische »Cocina Criolla« oder gar ein Barbecue zu erleben, kann den einstigen Hausherren verstehen: Zwei Monate Sommerferien auf La Paz sind wirklich das absolute Minimum.

Buchtipp: »Das Aleph« von Jorge Luis Borges

Être l'hôte du président

« Mon engagement politique ne m'a jamais détourné d'une routine devenue chère à mes yeux : passer au moins deux mois à La Paz tous les étés. » Ces lignes viennent de la plume de Julio Argentino Roca, président de l'Argentine de 1880 à 1886 et de 1898 à 1904, et membre du groupe politique intellectuel «Generación del 80», qui misait sur l'immigration, la croissance économique et une classe moyenne forte. Ces messieurs ne discutaient pas seulement leurs réformes dans la capitale, à Buenos Aires, mais aussi à 110 kilomètres de là, à Ascochinga, dans la maison de campagne du président. Pour Julio Argentino Roca, La Paz était à la fois une résidence d'été et un lieu de rencontre pour politiciens. L'Estancia dégage aujourd'hui encore cette atmosphère. L'hôte réside dans des bâtiments peints en jaune et restaurés avec amour dans le style colonial et de la Renaissance italienne. Il peut flâner dans l'immense parc aménagé par le paysagiste français Charles Thays ou plonger dans la piscine qui, sur la demande de Roca, fut la première de toute l'Argentine à être de dimension olympique. La vie de campagne est luxueuse à La Paz : il n'y manque ni les deux terrains de polo, où se déroulent les compétitions nationales, ni le golf à 18 trous, dont chaque brin d'herbe semble avoir été coupé au ciseau à ongles par le greenkeeper en personne. Si après une partie, on a encore la chance de déguster la typique «cocina criolla» ou un barbecue au restaurant, on peut alors comprendre le maître de maison de jadis : deux mois d'été à La Paz sont le strict minimum.

Livre à emporter : « L'Aleph » de Jorge Luis Borges

ANREISE	50 Kilometer nordöstlich des Flughafens Córdoba gelegen (dorthin Inlandsflüge ab Buenos Aires)
PREISE	$
ZIMMER	2 Dreibettzimmer, 19 Doppelzimmer, 1 Präsidentensuite
KÜCHE	Regionale Spezialitäten (Cocina Criolla) und typisch argentinisches Barbecue (Asado)
GESCHICHTE	Aus dem einstigen Landsitz des Präsidenten wurde ein luxuriöses Landhotel
X-FAKTOR	Sommerfrische auf staatsmännische Art

ACCÈS	Situé à 50 kilomètres au nord-est de l'aéroport de Córdoba (vols intérieurs depuis Buenos Aires)
PRIX	$
CHAMBRES	2 chambres à trois lits, 19 chambres doubles, 1 suite présidentielle
RESTAURATION	Spécialités régionales (cocina criolla) et barbecue typiquement argentin (asado)
HISTOIRE	L'ancienne résidence du président a été transformée en hôtel luxueux
LE « PETIT PLUS »	Passer l'été comme un chef d'État

A good vintage...
Estancia Ancón, Mendoza

A good vintage

Mendoza is in the Cuyo region in western Argentina and lies at the foot of the Andean Cordilleras. In the language of the indigenous peoples, "Cuyo" means "sandy soil", but don't let that fool you: with more than 300 days of sunshine a year, and sophisticated irrigation systems, Cuyo is a green and blossoming wonderland renowned throughout the world for its exceptional wines. One of its finest producers is the Estancia Ancón. The ivy-clad château, with its crannied architecture, vaulted ceilings, and round tower, would look more in place among the vineyards of France, you'd think, than in the rolling empty spaces of Argentina. And you wouldn't be too wrong, since the owners originally haled from Limoges and came to Mendoza in 1760. The Bombal family still manage the estate to this day – Lucila Bombal and her children keep a watchful eye on the wine-making to ensure that, for all the modern methods of production, the old vintner traditions are upheld. Since 1999 the Bombals have been taking guests at the château too: every year, from mid October to early May, connoisseurs of wine and of natural beauty move in to the six hotel rooms, which have dark gleaming parquet floors, furniture with a touch of the aristocratic, and a sparing deployment of knick-knacks. Vineyard trips and tastings are on offer, alongside walks amid the walnut and cherry orchards of the estate, or horse riding with the snow-capped Andes to marvel at. In the evenings, good home cooking is served, using produce mainly from the estate and washed down, of course, with estate wines.

Book to pack: "The Winners" by Julio Cortázar

Estancia Ancón

San José, Tupungato

5500 Mendoza

Argentina

Tel. (54) 261488245

Tel. for bookings (54) 2614200037

E-mail: bombal@arnet.com.ar

Website: www.estanciancon.com

www.great-escapes-hotels.com

DIRECTIONS	Situated 80 minutes by road southwest of Mendoza international airport (domestic flights from Buenos Aires), at an altitude of 1,300 metres/approx. 4,000 feet
RATES	$$$
ROOMS	5 double rooms and 1 single room. Open from 15 October to 1 May
FOOD	Regional specialities using estate produce and served with estate wines
HISTORY	The summer residence of the Bombals, built in 1933, has been a small hotel since 1999
X-FACTOR	French-cum-South American style, and first-class wines

Ein guter Jahrgang

Mendoza gehört zur Region Cuyo – im Westen Argentiniens und am Fuß der Andenkordillere gelegen. In der Sprache der Ureinwohner bedeutet Cuyo so viel wie »sandige Erde«, doch davon sollte man sich nicht täuschen lassen: Mehr als 300 Sonnentage im Jahr und ausgefeilte Bewässerungssysteme verwandeln Cuyo in ein blühendes und grünes Wunderland, das in aller Welt für seine ausgezeichneten Weine berühmt ist. Zu den besten Produzenten gehört die Estancia Ancón – mit ihrem Château unter einer dichten Efeudecke, das man ob seiner verwinkelten Architektur, seiner Gewölbedecken und seines Rundturms eher in Frankreichs Rebbergen als in der Weite Argentiniens vermuten würde. Dieser Eindruck kommt nicht von ungefähr, denn die Besitzer stammen ursprünglich aus Limoges und kamen anno 1760 nach Mendoza. Die Familie Bombal managt das Gut noch heute – Lucila Bombal und ihre Kinder wachen strengstens darüber, dass trotz moderner Produktionstechniken die alten Winzertraditionen erhalten bleiben. Seit 1999 empfangen die Bombals im Schloss auch Gäste: Jedes Jahr zwischen Mitte Oktober und Anfang Mai ziehen Wein- und Naturliebhaber in die sechs Hotelzimmer, die mit dunkel glänzendem Parkett, aristokratisch angehauchten Möbeln und ohne viel Nippes ausgestattet sind. Neben Ausflügen in die Rebberge und Degustationen stehen Spaziergänge über das herrliche Gelände voller Walnuss- und Kirschbäume auf dem Programm sowie Ausritte vor der Kulisse der schneebedeckten Anden. Abends verwöhnt man die Besucher mit Hausmannskost, für die hauptsächlich Produkte aus eigenem Anbau verwendet und die natürlich von eigenen Weinen begleitet werden.

Buchtipp: »Die Gewinner« von Julio Cortázar

Un bon cru

Située dans l'Ouest de l'Argentine au pied de la cordillère des Andes, Mendoza se trouve dans la région de Cuyo. Dans le dialecte indigène Cuyo signifie « terre de sable », mais ne nous laissons pas abuser par ce terme. En effet, plus de 300 jours de soleil par an et un judicieux système d'irrigation ont métamorphosé Cuyo en une région verdoyante connue dans le monde entier pour la qualité de ses vins. Estancia Ancón compte parmi les meilleurs producteurs, et quand on regarde son château recouvert d'une épaisse couche de lierre, avec ses plafonds voûtés et son donjon, on l'imaginerait plus dans les vignobles de France que sur les vastes étendues de l'Argentine. Cette impression n'est pas complètement fausse car les premiers propriétaires, qui arrivèrent à Mendoza en 1760, étaient originaires de Limoges. La famille Bombal gère son exploitation aujourd'hui encore – Lucila Bombal et ses enfants veillent au respect des traditions tout en employant des techniques de production modernes. Depuis 1999, le château reçoit aussi des hôtes : tous les ans, entre la mi-octobre et début mai, les amateurs de vin et de nature peuvent résider dans l'une des six chambres décorées sobrement, avec parquet ciré et meubles aristocratiques. À côté des excursions dans les vignobles et des dégustations, le château propose des promenades dans la magnifique propriété, où poussent une multitude de noyers et de cerisiers, ainsi que des randonnées à cheval avec pour décor les sommets neigeux des Andes. Le soir on flatte les papilles des hôtes avec une cuisine rustique, préparée principalement avec des produits maisons et accompagnée bien sûr des vins des vignobles alentour.

Livre à emporter : « Les gagnants » de Julio Cortázar

ANREISE	80 Fahrtminuten südwestlich des Internationalen Flughafens Mendoza gelegen (dorthin Inlandsflüge ab Buenos Aires), auf 1.300 Metern Höhe
PREISE	$$$
ZIMMER	5 Doppelzimmer und 1 Einzelzimmer. Für Gäste geöffnet vom 15. Oktober bis 1. Mai
KÜCHE	Regionale Spezialitäten aus eigenem Anbau und Weine aus eigener Produktion
GESCHICHTE	Der 1933 erbaute Sommersitz der Bombals ist seit 1999 ein kleines Hotel
X-FAKTOR	Französisch-südamerikanisches Flair und 1A-Weine

ACCÈS	Situé à 80 minutes en voiture au sud-ouest de l'aéroport international de Mendoza (vols intérieurs depuis Buenos Aires), à une altitude de 1.300 mètres
PRIX	$$$
CHAMBRES	5 chambres doubles et 1 chambre simple. Hôtellerie ouverte du 15 octobre au 1er mai
RESTAURATION	Spécialités régionales maisons
HISTOIRE	La résidence d'été des Bombal, construite en 1933, a été transformée en un petit hôtel en 1999
LE « PETIT PLUS »	Ambiance franco-sud-américaine et vins de première classe

A literary trip...
Los Álamos, Mendoza

Los Alamos, Mendoza

A literary trip

"She is wherever there is music and the gentle blue of the sky" – thus wrote Argentina's most famous writer, Jorge Luis Borges, of his fellow writer Susana Bombal. Today you can see for yourself just how close the two were to each other – at Los Alamos, once the country residence of Bombal. About 1920 she became the owner of this venerable old family property in the midst of the Mendoza wine-growing district, and transformed it into a meeting place for the intelligentsia. It was a favourite place not only for Jorge Luis Borges but also for Silvina Ocampo (one of the leading women poets) and Manuel Mujica Láinez, who achieved fame as a journalist on the daily *La Nación* – both regularly spent weekends at Los Alamos. To this day the cosy rooms can be seen where this circle once gathered, and you can browse in the substantial library or see where Susana Bombal wrote the majority of her works, or admire paintings by Borges' sister Norah. The interior décor emphasizes a personal, country style, with terracotta hues, delicately painted tiles, and dark furniture. It has just five guest rooms – but they are opulent, and one even boasts a billiards table. When you are resident here, you will be spoilt with traditional Argentine fare, but you'll also have ample opportunity to work off any surplus calories. There are walks to be taken through the surrounding vineyards, there's trout fishing and duck shooting, and there's horse riding in the Andes. And if you're in for adventures on water, there's rafting in the nearby canyons. And finally, if relaxing with an evening's musical entertainment is your preference, Los Alamos offers Argentine barbecues followed by dancing.

Book to pack: "Selected Poems" by Jorge Luis Borges

Los Alamos
San Rafael
Mendoza
Argentina
Tel. (54) 2627 442350
Fax (54) 2627 426858
E-mail: info@pagosargentinos.com
Website: www.fincalosalamos.com
www.great-escapes-hotels.com

DIRECTIONS	Situated 200 km/125 miles south of Mendoza airport (regular domestic flights from Buenos Aires)
RATES	$$$
ROOMS	5 double rooms
FOOD	Mouth-watering home cooking following old family recipes
HISTORY	Built in 1830, the property was formerly the country residence of writer Susana Bombal. It is still family owned
X-FACTOR	Life in the country, pure and simple – just as Argentina's novelists describe it

Eine literarische Reise

»Sie ist dort, wo Musik ist und das sanfte Blau des Himmels« – das schrieb Argentiniens berühmtester Autor Jorge Luis Borges über seine Kollegin Susana Bombal. Wie nahe sich die beiden standen, kann man heute noch nachvollziehen – in Los Alamos, dem einstigen Landsitz der Schriftstellerin. Mitten in der Weinregion Mendoza übernahm Susana Bombal um 1920 den altehrwürdigen Familienbesitz und verwandelte ihn in einen Treffpunkt der Intellektuellen. Hier fand nicht nur Jorge Luis Borges einen seiner Lieblingsplätze; auch Silvina Ocampo (»Gedichte einer verzweifelten Liebe«) und Manuel Mujica Láinez, der als Journalist der Tageszeitung »La Nación« berühmt wurde, verbrachten regelmäßig ihr Wochenende auf Los Alamos. Noch heute kann man die gemütlichen Räume besichtigen, in denen sich die Zirkel einst trafen, sich durch die gut sortierte Bibliothek lesen, einen Blick in das Zimmer werfen, in dem Susana Bombal die meisten ihrer Werke schrieb, oder Gemälde von Borges' Schwester Norah bewundern. Das Haus ist im persönlichen Countrystil ausgestattet, setzt auf Terrakottatöne, filigran bemalte Fliesen und dunkle Möbel und besitzt nur fünf opulente Gästezimmer (in einem prangt sogar ein Billardtisch). Wer hier wohnt, wird mit argentinischer Hausmannskost nach überlieferten Rezepten verwöhnt, hat aber reichlich Gelegenheit, die Kalorien wieder abzutrainieren. Zur Auswahl stehen Spaziergänge durch die umliegenden Weinberge, Forellenfischen und die Entenjagd oder Ausritte in die Anden. Wer Wasser nicht scheut, kann zudem durch die nahen Canyons raften; und für alle, die am liebsten bei Musik entspannen, bietet Los Alamos argentinische Grillabende mit anschließendem Tanz.

Buchtipp: »Der Geschmack eines Apfels« von Jorge Luis Borges

Un voyage littéraire

« Elle est là où sont la musique et le bleu du ciel », a écrit Jorge Luis Borges, l'auteur le plus célèbre d'Argentine, sur sa collègue Susana Bombal. Leur complicité mutuelle se constate aujourd'hui encore, à Los Alamos, l'ancienne résidence de la femme écrivain. En 1920, Susana Bombal reprit la propriété familiale située en pleine région viticole pour la transformer en lieu de rencontre des intellectuels. Ce fut l'endroit préféré de Jorge Luis Borges. Quant à Silvina Ocampo (« Poèmes d'amour désespéré ») et Manuel Mujica Láinez, célèbre journaliste du quotidien « La Nación », ils passaient tous leurs week-ends à Los Alamos. De nos jours on peut encore visiter les pièces confortables où les membres du cercle se réunissaient, lire les ouvrages de la bibliothèque, jeter un regard dans le bureau où Susana Bombal a écrit la plupart de ses livres ou admirer les tableaux de Norah, la sœur de Borges. La maison est décorée dans un style country personnel, affectionne les tons de terre cuite, le carrelage finement peint et les meubles sombres, et elle possède cinq chambres d'hôtes généreuses où trône même dans l'une d'elles une table de billard. Celui qui réside ici aura le plaisir de trouver une gastronomie argentine préparée selon des recettes traditionnelles. Mais n'ayez crainte, vous aurez amplement l'occasion de brûler vos calories. La maison propose au choix des promenades dans les vignobles alentour, la pêche à la truite, la chasse au canard ou des randonnées à cheval dans les Andes. Ceux qui ne craignent pas l'eau pourront faire du rafting dans les proches canyons et pour tous ceux qui préfèrent se détendre avec de la musique, Los Alamos offre des soirées dansantes commençant par un barbecue argentin.

Livre à emporter : « L'art de poésie » de Jorge Luis Borges

ANREISE	200 Kilometer südlich des Flughafens Mendoza gelegen (dorthin regelmäßige Inlandsflüge ab Buenos Aires)
PREISE	$$$
ZIMMER	5 Doppelzimmer
KÜCHE	Traumhafte Hausmannskost nach alten Familienrezepten
GESCHICHTE	1830 erbaut und ehemaliger Landsitz der Schriftstellerin Susana Bombal. Noch heute in Familienbesitz
X-FAKTOR	Landleben pur – so schön wie in argentinischen Romanen

ACCÈS	Situé à 200 kilomètres au sud de l'aéroport de Mendoza (vols intérieurs réguliers depuis Buenos Aires)
PRIX	$$$
CHAMBRES	5 chambres doubles
CUISINE	Merveilleuse cuisine maison selon de vieilles recettes de famille
HISTOIRE	Construite en 1830, c'est l'ancienne résidence de l'écrivain Susana Bombal. Se trouve aujourd'hui encore en possession de la famille
LE « PETIT PLUS »	La vie à la campagne par excellence – aussi belle que dans les romans argentins

A natural beauty...
La Becasina Delta Lodge, Province Buenos Aires

La Becasina Delta Lodge, Province Buenos Aires

A natural beauty

Amazing to think town and country can be so close and yet
so far apart: just a few miles out of Buenos Aires you come
to the Paraná delta, an enchanting landscape of small water-
ways and lush vegetation, where life seems to move in slow
motion, as if bedded on velvet. It's the perfect place to while
away the days paddling a kayak on the river, watching the
birds and listening to their shrill, wondrous calls, or fishing
from the riverbank in a mood so peaceful that bristling
appointments diaries and ceaselessly jangling mobiles seem
a world away. In the heart of this idyllic realm, La Becasina
Delta Lodge awaits its guests. It's situated on the bank of the
Arroyo Las Cañas, with marshlands around it that have largely remained unspoilt. The few stray buildings supported
on stilts seem almost to hover above the water, and are linked by wooden walkways or bridges. Every one of the 15 bungalow suites has all the charisma of a private residence – for
a few happy days, you are the owner of a humble lodging of
understated luxury, with a dream veranda and views of the
greenery. If you don't only want to admire the water from
a dry haven, why not take time out on the river in a boat,
or indeed *in* it? The only imperative rule is always to swim
against the current – otherwise you'll be borne away from
paradise all too swiftly...

**Book to pack: "Mascaro, the American Hunter"
by Haroldo Conti**

La Becasina Delta Lodge	
Arroyo Las Cañas	
2da Sección de Islas del Delta/San Fernando	
Buenos Aires	
Argentina	
Tel. (54) 1143282687	
Fax (54) 1147282070	
E-mail: reservas@labecasina.com	
Website: www.labecasina.com	
www.great-escapes-hotels.com	

DIRECTIONS	Situated some 60 km/38 miles north of Buenos Aires. One-hour boat transfer from San Fernando/Tigre US$ 30 per person
RATES	$$
ROOMS	15 bungalow suites for 2 people
FOOD	Argentine specialities and wines
HISTORY	Opened 1st April 2001
X-FACTOR	Everything is in flow – feel good by the water

Natürlich schön

So nahe können Stadt und Land nebeneinander liegen und so fern können sich beide Welten sein: Man muss nur ein paar Kilometer aus Buenos Aires hinausfahren und schon erreicht man das Paraná-Delta, eine Märchenlandschaft mit kleinen Wasserwegen und üppiger Vegetation, in der das Leben noch in Zeitlupe und wie unter Samt gelegen abläuft. Hier kann man seine Tage damit verbringen, mit dem Kajak auf den Fluss hinaus zu paddeln, den Vögeln hinterher zu sehen und ihren schrill-schönen Rufen zu lauschen oder mit so viel Seelenruhe am Ufer zu angeln, als hätte man niemals Wochen voller berstender Terminkalender und im Sekundentakt klingelnder Handys erlebt. Inmitten dieses Idylls wartet die La Becasina Delta Lodge auf Gäste – am Ufer des Arroyo Las Cañas gelegen und um sich herum eine Sumpflandschaft, die ihren ursprünglichen Charakter noch weitgehend erhalten konnte. Die einzelnen Gebäude scheinen auf ihren Stelzen über dem Wasser zu schweben und sind über hölzerne Stege oder Brücken miteinander verbunden. Jede der 15 Bungalow-Suiten besitzt das Flair einer Privatadresse – für ein paar glückliche Tage ist man Besitzer eines Häuschens mit dezentem Luxus und einer traumhaften Veranda mit Blick ins Grüne. Wer das Wasser nicht nur vom Trockenen aus bewundern will, kann an Bootsausflügen teilnehmen oder ganz einfach im Fluss untertauchen. Dabei gilt nur eine einzige Regel: Immer gegen die Strömung schwimmen – sonst wird man allzu schnell vom Paradies weggetrieben.

Buchtipp: »Op Oloop« von Juan Filloy

Des vacances au naturel

Buenos Aires, la capitale trépidante, ne se trouve qu'à quelques kilomètres, et pourtant elle semble très loin d'ici. En fait nous sommes dans un autre monde, celui du delta du Paraná, véritable paysage de contes de fées avec ses canaux et sa végétation luxuriante. Ici, la vie passe encore au ralenti, comme si elle glissait sur du velours. On peut passer ses journées en kayac sur le fleuve à regarder les oiseaux et écouter leurs beaux cris perçants ou pêcher sur les rives en toute sérénité. Envolés les agendas bourrés des semaines durant de rendez-vous urgents, oubliée la sonnerie incessante des portables.

Située sur la rive de l'Arroyo Las Cañas, entourée d'un paysage de marécages qui a su préserver son caractère original, la Becasina Delta Lodge attend ses hôtes pour partager avec eux ce site idyllique. Les constructions sur pilotis, reliées entre elles par des passerelles en bois et des pontons, semblent flotter au-dessus de l'eau. Chaque suite-bungalow a son caractère particulier – pendant quelques jours, on sera l'heureux propriétaire d'une maisonnette au luxe sobre dotée d'une véranda de rêve s'ouvrant sur la verdure. Et ceux qui ne veulent pas se contenter d'admirer l'eau de loin peuvent participer à des sorties en bateau ou tout simplement se baigner, en veillant cependant à nager contre le courant – sinon ils seraient trop vite entraînés loin de ce paradis.

Livre à emporter : « La ballade du peuplier carolin » de Haroldo Conti

ANREISE	Rund 60 Kilometer nördlich von Buenos Aires gelegen. Einstündiger Bootstransfer ab San Fernando/Tigre US$ 30 pro Person
PREISE	$$
ZIMMER	15 Bungalow-Suiten für je 2 Personen
KÜCHE	Argentinische Spezialitäten und Weine
GESCHICHTE	Am 1. April 2001 eröffnet
X-FAKTOR	Alles fließt – Wohlfühlen am Wasser

ACCÈS	Situé à 60 kilomètres au nord de Buenos Aires. À une heure de bateau de San Fernando/Tigre, US$ 30 par personne
PRIX	$$
CHAMBRES	15 suites-bungalows pour 2 personnes
RESTAURATION	Spécialités et vins argentins
HISTOIRE	Ouvert le 1er avril 2001
LE « PETIT PLUS »	Au fil de l'eau

Perfection of form...
La Escondida, Province Buenos Aires

La Escondida,
Province Buenos Aires

Perfection of form

For Paul Pieres, memories of his childhood and youth in
the pampas of Argentina are inseparable from polo. The
moment he and his five siblings got out of school, they sadd-
led their horses and rode out onto the pitch to thwack balls.
"My father always had five or six horses in the stables and
we kept those poor animals pretty busy," laughs Paul Pieres,
looking back, "but they loved polo as much as we did!"
Nowadays he shares his delight in Argentina's favourite
sport with visitors from all around the world. Four years
ago, with his wife Florencia, he opened the Estancia La
Escondida. It is not only one of the best places for polo
around Buenos Aires, it is also an architectural achievement
of high interest. The sandstone-coloured building seems to
have been set down amid the trees and greenery, clear and
simple of line, wholly unornamented. The lofty interior
spaces with their wooden ceilings and sparing, stylish furni-
shings convey an airy sense of spaciousness – and warm
tones to offset the stone colours are provided by the open
fire, colourful throws, and hides. Modern design is combined with nature without any sense of strain, and gives
guests the experience of an all-in work of art – whether it's
for a weekend escape from the city or for a whole month
(La Escondida offers polo programmes up to four weeks).
Of course the best place to relax after a day in the saddle is
beside the pool, from where you can enjoy evening views
of the most glorious sunsets Argentina has to offer.
Book to pack: "The Tunnel" by Ernesto Sabato

La Escondida
Pilar/Buenos Aires
Argentina
Tel. (54) 2322400588
E-mail: info@paulpieres.com
Website: www.estancialaescondida.com.ar
www.great-escapes-hotels.com

DIRECTIONS	Situated 60 km/39 miles (50 minutes by road) northwest of Buenos Aires
RATES	$$
ROOMS	8 suites
FOOD	Home cooking using produce from the estate or region. Delicious "asados" (barbecues)
HISTORY	A country hotel in modern design, opened in 2000
X-FACTOR	For those who love active holidays and architecture

Formvollendet

Für Paul Pieres ist die Erinnerung an seine Kindheit und Jugend in der argentinischen Pampa untrennbar mit dem Polospiel verbunden: Sobald er und seine fünf Geschwister aus der Schule kamen, sattelten sie die Pferde, ritten aufs Feld und schlugen die Bälle um die Wette. »Mein Vater hatte immer fünf oder sechs Pferde im Stall, und wir hielten die armen Tiere ziemlich auf Trab«, lacht Paul Pieres heute, »aber sie mochten Polo genau so gern wie wir!« Den Spaß an Argentiniens beliebtester Sportart bringt er inzwischen auch Gästen aus aller Welt näher. Zusammen mit seiner Frau Florencia hat er vor vier Jahren die Estancia La Escondida eröffnet. Sie gehört nicht nur zu den besten Polo-Adressen rund um Buenos Aires, sondern ist zugleich ein architektonischer Höhepunkt: Der sandsteinfarbene Bau wurde wie ein Würfel aufs Grün und zwischen mächtige Bäume gesetzt; klar, einfach und schnörkellos inszeniert. Im Inneren vermitteln hohe Räume mit Holzdecken und sparsam-eleganter Möblierung viel Luft und Weite – für warme Akzente inmitten all der Steintöne sorgen Kaminfeuer, bunte Decken und Felle. Modernes Design soll sich hier wie selbstverständlich mit der Natur verbinden und Besucher in ein Gesamtkunstwerk entführen – sei es nur für ein Wochenende fern der Großstadt oder gleich für einen ganzen Monat (La Escondida bietet bis zu vierwöchige Polo-Programme an). Der schönste Platz nach einem Tag im Sattel ist übrigens ein Sessel am Pool: Von dort aus genießt man abends einen fantastischen Blick über das lang gezogene Becken mit offener Feuerstelle und hinein in einen der kitschig-schönsten Sonnenuntergänge, den Argentinien zu bieten hat.

Buchtipp: »Stefanos weite Reise« von Maria T. Andruetto

Un parcours sans fautes

Lorsque Paul Pieres évoque ses jeunes années dans la pampa argentine, le souvenir du polo lui vient immédiatement à l'esprit. À peine rentrés de l'école, les enfants sellaient leurs chevaux, galopaient sur le terrain et c'est à celui qui marquerait le plus de buts. « Mon père avait toujours cinq ou six chevaux à l'écurie et nous ne les ménagions pas, les pauvres », dit-il en riant, « mais ils aimaient cela autant que nous ! » Aujourd'hui, il tente de communiquer l'amour de ce sport, le plus apprécié en Argentine, à des hôtes venus du monde entier. Il y a quatre ans, avec son épouse Florencia, il a ouvert l'Estancia La Escondida, une des meilleures adresses des environs de Buenos Aires pour les amateurs de polo, mais aussi un triomphe architectural : le bâtiment couleur de sable est posé comme un dé sur la verdure entre des arbres imposants – une mise en scène claire, simple, sans fioriture. À l'intérieur, des pièces hautes dotées de plafonds de bois et de quelques meubles élégants génèrent une ambiance aérée et spacieuse – les flammes dans la cheminée, des plaids multicolores et des fourrures posent quelques accents chauds sur les teintes terreuses.

Le design moderne doit se marier ici à la nature comme si cela allait de soi et entraîner les visiteurs dans une œuvre d'art totale – pour le temps d'un week-end ou d'un mois (La Escondida offre des programmes de polo qui durent jusqu'à quatre semaines). Après une journée en selle, il fait bon se reposer sur un fauteuil près de la piscine. Le soir on jouit ici d'une vue fantastique sur le bassin qui s'étire en longueur et sur l'un des plus beaux couchers de soleil bigarrés que l'Argentine ait à offrir.

Livre à emporter : « Le tunnel », d'Ernesto Sabato

ANREISE	60 Kilometer (50 Fahrtminuten) nordwestlich von Buenos Aires gelegen
PREISE	$$
ZIMMER	8 Suiten
KÜCHE	Hausgemachte Gerichte mit Zutaten aus eigenem Anbau oder der Region. Köstliche »asados« (Barbecues)
GESCHICHTE	Modern designtes Landhotel, 2000 eröffnet
X-FAKTOR	Für Aktivurlauber und Architekturliebhaber

ACCÈS	Situé à 60 kilomètres (50 minutes en voiture) au nord-ouest de Buenos Aires
PRIX	$$
CHAMBRES	8 suites
RESTAURATION	Plats cuisinés sur place avec produits du jardin ou de la région. «Asados» (barbecues) succulents
HISTOIRE	Hôtel de campagne au design moderne, ouvert en 2000
LE « PETIT PLUS »	Pour les amateurs d'exercice et d'architecture

Rooms with a family connect

Estancia El Rosario de Areco, Province Buenos Aires

Rooms with a family connection

For Juan Francisco Guevara and his wife Florencia, family is the main thing in life. The owners of El Rosario de Areco have nine children and four grandchildren – and like to have them around as much as possible. So their estancia truly is a family business. The six sons in particular do sterling work at this hotel 115 kilometres (75 miles) from Buenos Aires, seeing to guests from all over the world who've come to enjoy the Argentine countryside. This being horse-crazy Argentina, there are special pleasures to indulge in too: El Rosario de Areco is a famed polo club with two pitches of its own and even its own team, which turns out to regional and national tournaments. If you feel like a go at smashing the ball across the grass without falling out of the saddle yourself, you can take private tuition from professional jockeys here or even book a whole week's polo. For everyone else, the estancia does arrange horse riding of the usual kind, or you can take walks around the estate or head for a dip in the pool. The house itself is in a modern, plain country style, with walls in warm natural hues, soft inviting sofas by the fireside, and sturdy stoneware all contributing to that authentic country house feel. The genuine home cooking is in tune with the atmosphere – from fresh milk at breakfast to plaited loaves warm from the oven in the afternoon to grilled beef in the evening. This is an estancia not just for private vacationers: El Rosario de Areco also offers events and incentives for companies: car manufacturers, universities, and banks from around the world have already used the facilities.

Book to pack: "A Change of Light and Other Stories" by Julio Cortázar

---

Estancia El Rosario de Areco
Casilla de Correo 85
2760 San Antonio de Areco
Argentina
Tel. (54) 2326 451000
Website: www.rosariodeareco.com.ar
www.great-escapes-hotels.com

DIRECTIONS	Situated 115 km/75 miles northwest of Buenos Aires
RATES	$$$
ROOMS	14 Suites, 1 Senior Suite
FOOD	Hearty home cooking
HISTORY	A country residence built in 1892, converted into a hotel
X-FACTOR	A riding holiday for all the family – with a whole family

Zimmer mit Familienanschluss

Für Juan Francisco Guevara und seine Frau Florencia ist die Familie das Wichtigste. Neun Kinder und vier Enkel haben die Besitzer von El Rosario de Areco – und alle am liebsten so oft wie möglich um sich herum. Deshalb ist ihre Estancia auch ein echter Familienbetrieb. Vor allem die sechs Söhne kümmern sich im Hotel um die Gäste aus aller Welt, die hier, 115 Kilometer von Buenos Aires entfernt, argentinische Landluft schnuppern wollen. Durch diese weht im pferde-verrückten Argentinien vor allem Stallduft: El Rosario de Areco besitzt als renommierter Polo-Club zwei eigene Spiel-felder und sogar eine eigene Mannschaft, die bei regionalen und nationalen Turnieren antritt. Wer es den Männern nach-machen und den Ball möglichst ohne aus dem Sattel zu fal-len über den Rasen schlagen will, kann hier Privatstunden bei professionellen Jockeys nehmen oder gleich eine ganze Polo-Woche buchen. Für alle anderen organisiert die Estan-cia aber auch ganz normale Ausritte oder Spaziergänge durch den umliegenden Park und lässt sie anschließend im Pool untertauchen. Das Haus selbst bietet modernen und schlichten Countrystil; in warmen Naturtönen getünchte Wände, kuschelige Sofas am Kamin und robustes Steingut sorgen für unverfälschtes Landhaus-Flair. Passend dazu setzt die Küche auf echte Hausmannskost – inklusive fri-scher Milch zum Frühstück, ofenwarmen Hefezöpfen am Nachmittag und gegrilltem Rind am Abend. Auf den Ge-schmack sind übrigens nicht nur Privaturlauber gekommen: El Rosario de Areco veranstaltet auch Events oder Incentives für Firmen; zu Gast waren bereits internationale Auto-häuser, Universitäten und Banken.

Buchtipp: »Passatwinde« von Julio Cortázar

Être accueilli dans une famille

Pour Juan Francisco Guevara et sa femme Frau Florencia la famille est la chose la plus importante. Il faut dire aussi que les propriétaires d'El Rosario de Areco ont neuf enfants et quatre petits-enfants et ce qu'ils préfèrent, c'est les avoir auprès d'eux le plus souvent possible. Leur Estancia est donc une véritable exploitation familiale. Les fils surtout s'occupent des clients du monde entier qui, à cent quinze kilomètres de Buenos Aires, désirent respirer un peu de la campagne argentine. Mais c'est aussi l'air des écuries que l'on sent dans cette Argentine éperdument éprise de chevaux : en tant que club de polo de grande renommée, El Rosario de Areco possède deux terrains et même une équipe qui dispute des tournois régionaux et internationaux. Celui qui veut imiter les joueurs et courir après la balle sans tom-ber de cheval peut prendre des cours particuliers auprès de jockeys professionnels ou réserver directement toute une semaine de polo. Pour tous les autres l'Estancia organise aussi des promenades à pied ou à cheval dans le parc, et propose sa piscine pour se détendre. La maison est décorée dans un style campagnard sobre et moderne. Les murs badi-geonnés dans des tons chauds et naturels, les canapés moel-leux près de la cheminée, les objets en grès dégagent une atmosphère authentique de maison de campagne. En accord avec cela, la cuisine mise sur les plats rustiques, y compris le lait qui vient d'être trait au petit déjeuner, les pains brio-chés sortis tout droit du four l'après-midi et le bœuf grillé le soir. Les touristes ne sont pas les seuls à goûter toutes ces joies : El Rosario de Areco organise aussi des journées spé-ciales pour les sociétés. Des compagnies de voitures, des universités et des banques du monde entier ont déjà été leurs hôtes.

Livre à emporter : « Le fantastique argentin » de Julio Cortázar

ANREISE	115 Kilometer nordwestlich von Buenos Aires gelegen	ACCÈS	Situé à 115 kilomètres au nord-ouest de Buenos Aires
PREISE	$$$	PRIX	$$$
ZIMMER	14 Suiten, 1 Senior Suite	CHAMBRES	14 suites, 1 Senior Suite
KÜCHE	Herzhaft und hausgemacht	RESTAURATION	Savoureuse cuisine maison
GESCHICHTE	Ein 1892 errichteter Landsitz wurde zum Hotel umgebaut	HISTOIRE	Maison de campagne construite en 1892, puis trans-formée en hôtel
X-FAKTOR	Reiterferien für die ganze Familie – bei einer ganzen Familie	LE « PETIT PLUS »	Vacances d'équitation pour toute la famille et chez une famille

King for a day...
Estancia La Candelaria, Province Buenos Aires

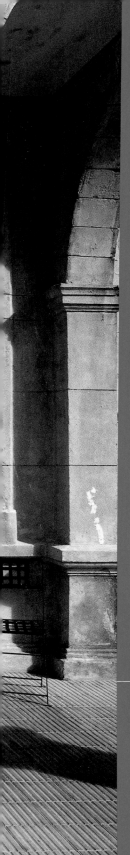

King for a day

At first glance you'd think this castle with its turrets, battlements, and high windows belonged in the Loire Valley, or maybe Eurodisney near Paris – if it weren't for the fact that it's in this breathtaking tropical garden. More than 240 different trees and plants grow here, such as palms, eucalyptus trees, or banana plants. A gleaming white bridge spans a modest watercourse, and the grass shines as if it had been sprayed with bright green paint. The park was created by the famous landscape architect Charles Thays, and the château fits into it perfectly. The residence was built in the mid-19th century by pharmacist and sheep breeder Don Orestes Piñeiro, who named it after his wife, Doña Candelaria Del Marmol. La Candelaria was the family's other world, their retreat in the solitude of the Argentine pampas, far from civilisation. And although the region is now perfectly accessible, and anything but backwoods, the château remains a quiet refuge to get away to. You reside in spacious rooms beneath coffered ceilings and crystal chandeliers. The floors are gleaming parquet or costly carpet, the armchairs are carved, and the beds have gilded bedsteads. La Candelaria is a return to a magnificent era long thought forgotten, and guests here can be king for a while. The pastimes all strike the right note of class, among them billiards, tennis, golf, and polo. The property still belongs to the same family, and while the owners may be deeply attached to the past, they also have a real sense of the present: all the sporting and leisure activities are included in the room price. This is Argentina all inclusive.

Book to pack: "Voices" by Antonio Porchia

Estancia La Candelaria

Ruta 205, km 114.5

Lobos, Peia de Buenos Aires

Argentina

Tel. (54) 2227 424404

Fax (54) 2227 494132

E-mail: info@estanciacandelaria.com

Website: www.estanciacandelaria.com

www.great-escapes-hotels.com

DIRECTIONS	Situated 115 km/75 miles northeast of Buenos Aires.
RATES	$$$
ROOMS	2 double rooms in bungalows, 1 double in the old mill, 2 double in the Casa del Sol, 8 double in colonial houses, 10 double and 2 suites in the château
FOOD	Refined Argentine and international cuisine
HISTORY	A picture-book retreat, family-owned since 1840
X-FACTOR	My palace, my park, my polo pitch

Heute ein König

Auf den ersten Blick würde man dieses Schloss mit seinen
spitzen Türmen, Zinnen und hohen Fenstern eher im Tal
der Loire oder im Disneyland bei Paris vermuten – stünde
es nicht in diesem traumhaften tropischen Garten. Hier
gedeihen mehr als 240 verschiedene Pflanzen wie Palmen,
Eukalyptusbäume oder Bananenstauden, über einen kleinen
Wasserlauf spannt sich eine strahlend weiße Brücke, und
der Rasen leuchtet, als habe man ihn mit hellgrüner Farbe
besprüht. Der Park trägt die Handschrift des berühmten
Landschaftsarchitekten Charles Thays, und das Château
passt dazu wie das Tüpfelchen auf dem i. Mitte des 19. Jahrhunderts ließ der Apotheker und Schafzüchter Don Orestes
Piñeiro das Anwesen bauen und benannte es nach seiner
Frau, Doña Candelaria Del Marmol. Mit La Candelaria schuf
sich die Familie eine andere Welt – in der Einsamkeit der
argentinischen Pampa und fern jeglicher Zivilisation gelegen. Und obwohl die Region inzwischen gut erschlossen
und alles andere als hinterwäldlerisch ist, ist diese Adresse
noch immer ein Fluchtpunkt und ein ruhiges Refugium.
Hier residiert man in weiten Räumen unter Kassettendecken
oder Kristalllüstern, schreitet über glänzendes Parkett oder
wertvolle Teppiche, thront auf geschnitzten Lehnstühlen
oder in goldumrahmten Betten. La Candelaria lässt eine
prachtvolle und längst vergessen geglaubte Epoche wieder
aufleben und verwandelt seine Gäste in Schlossherren auf
Zeit. Zum standesgemäßen Vergnügen gehören auch Billard, Tennis, Golf und Polo – und dass die Besitzer (das
Areal ist immer noch in Familienbesitz) trotz aller Liebe zur
Vergangenheit längst in der Gegenwart angekommen sind,
zeigt sich daran, dass alle Sport- und Freizeitaktivitäten im
Zimmerpreis eingeschlossen sind: Das ist Argentinien *all
inclusive*.
Buchtipp: »Verlassene Stimmen« von Antonio Porchia

Se sentir comme un roi

On pourrait croire au premier abord que ce château avec ses
tours, ses créneaux et ses hautes fenêtres se trouve dans la
Vallée de la Loire ou à Dysneyland près de Paris, s'il n'était
pas entouré de ces merveilleux jardins tropicaux, dans lesquels poussent plus de 240 espèces différentes de plantes,
comme des palmiers, des eucalyptus et des bananiers. Un
pont d'un blanc éclatant passe au-dessus d'un petit cours
d'eau et la pelouse resplendit comme si on l'avait peinte de
couleur verte. Le parc porte la signature du célèbre paysagiste Charles Thays et s'accorde parfaitement avec le château. C'est au milieu du 19e siècle que l'apothicaire et éle-
veur de moutons Don Orestes Piñeiro fit construire sa
demeure et la baptisa d'après sa femme, Doña Candelaria
Del Marmol. Avec La Candelaria la famille s'est créé un
autre univers, dans la solitude de la pampa argentine et loin
de toute civilisation. Et même si la région est maintenant
bien développée et tout sauf sauvage, cette adresse demeure
encore un refuge tranquille. Ici, on réside dans de larges
pièces sous un plafond à cassettes et des lustres en cristal,
on marche sur un parquet reluisant ou des tapis précieux,
on trône sur des fauteuils en bois sculpté ou on se prélasse
dans des lits dorés. La Candelaria fait revivre une époque
somptueuse que l'on croyait depuis longtemps révolue et
transforme pour un temps ses hôtes en châtelains. Pour se
divertir dignement, on aura le choix entre le billard, le tennis, le golf et le polo. Malgré leur amour pour le passé, les
propriétaires (la résidence est encore aux mains de la famille) ont les deux pieds dans le présent et cela se voit dans le
fait que toutes les activités sportives ou non sont comprises
dans le prix de la chambre : c'est l'Argentine *all inclusive*.
Livre à emporter : « Voix abandonnées » d'Antonio Porchia

ANREISE	115 Kilometer nordöstlich von Buenos Aires gelegen
PREISE	$$$
ZIMMER	2 Doppelzimmer in Bungalows, 1 Doppelzimmer in der alten Mühle, 2 Doppelzimmer in der Casa del Sol, 8 Doppelzimmer in traditionellen Kolonialhäusern, 10 Doppelzimmer und 2 Suiten im Schloss
KÜCHE	Verfeinerte argentinische und internationale Küche
GESCHICHTE	Familienbesitz wie aus dem Bilderbuch – seit 1840
X-FAKTOR	Mein Palast, mein Park, mein Polo-Feld

ACCÈS	Situé à 115 kilomètres de Buenos Aires
PRIX	$$$
CHAMBRES	2 de chambres doubles en bungalow, 1 chambre double dans l'ancien moulin, 2 chambres doubles à la Casa del Sol, 8 chambres doubles dans les maisons coloniales traditionnelles, 10 chambres doubles et 2 suites au château
RESTAURATION	Cuisine argentine et internationale de qualité
HISTOIRE	Entre les mains de la famille depuis 1840
LE « PETIT PLUS »	Mon palais, mon parc, mon terrain de polo

Welcome to a fairy-tale worl

Estancia Santa Rita, Province Buenos Aires

Welcome to a fairy-tale world

There are more shades of green in the park than on any painter's palette. The trees, shrubs, and lawns are resplendent dark and pale greens, lime and emerald green, subtle and acid hues. Covering some 40 hectares, the estate is one of the biggest estancias in the region – and certainly the most fairy-tale. In the heart of the green gardens is the majestic main building of Santa Rita, a palace in rose and cream, richly embellished with arches, pillars, and turrets – an homage to the Spanish colonial era. It was in 1790 that the Ezcurra family erected the first building on a kind of defensive line around Buenos Aires; subsequently, Santa Rita passed to the province's Senator Antonio Carboni, who left no doubt about his proprietorial claims and founded the village of Carboni four kilometres (2.4 miles) from the residence. Today the estate belongs to a married couple, Isabel Duggan and Franklin Nüdemberg, and their six daughters – and since 1996 has been an enchanting country hotel. The interior betrays a fantastic mix of styles. There are salons richly finished with stucco, flowing fabrics, and four-poster beds; rooms with unplastered walls, ceilings of dark wood, and open fireplaces; and sparingly furnished winter gardens with nothing to distract the eye from the natural scene. No two rooms are alike, and every one tells its story, through details that can take days to strike a visitor. Santa Rita's magical garden is best discovered on foot or on horseback. Then in the evenings, relax with classical music and candlelight as you choose from Argentine menus – wherever possible the ingredients are the estate's own produce.

Book to pack: "The Kiss of the Spiderwoman" by Manuel Puig

Estancia Santa Rita

Carboni

Partido de Lobos, Buenos Aires

Argentina

Tel. (54) 2227 495026 and (54) 11 4804634

Fax (54) 11 48059652

E-mail: info@santa-rita.com.ar

Website: www.santa-rita.com.ar

www.great-escapes-hotels.com

DIRECTIONS	Situated 120 km/75 miles southwest of Buenos Aires (90 minutes by road)
RATES	$
ROOMS	9 double rooms
FOOD	Argentine and international specialities; many ingredients are the estate's own produce
HISTORY	Built in 1870; a hotel since 1996
X-FACTOR	The prettiest of style blends in a green setting

Willkommen im Märchen

Der Park besitzt mehr Grüntöne, als auf der Palette eines professionellen Malers Platz hätten. Bäume, Büsche und Rasen leuchten in Dunkel- und Hellgrün, in Lind- und Smaragdgrün, in Zart- und Giftgrün. Mit rund 40 Hektar Fläche ist das Anwesen eine der größten Estancias der Region – und in jedem Fall das märchenhafteste: Inmitten des grünen Gartens nämlich thront das Haupthaus von Santa Rita, ein Palast in Rosé und Crème, mit Bögen, Säulen und Türmchen reich verziert und eine Hommage an die spanisch geprägte Kolonialzeit. 1790 errichtete die Familie Ezcurra die ersten Gebäude auf einer Art Verteidigungslinie um Buenos Aires, später ging Santa Rita an den Provinzsenator Antonio Carboni über, der seine Besitzansprüche mehr als deutlich manifestierte und vier Kilometer vom Landsitz entfernt das Dörfchen Carboni gründete. Heute gehört das Anwesen dem Ehepaar Isabel Duggan und Franklin Nüdemberg sowie seinen sechs Töchtern – und ist seit 1996 ein verwunschenes Countryhotel. In seinem Inneren regiert ein fantastischer Stilmix. Da gibt es reich mit Stuck, fließenden Stoffen und Himmelbetten ausgestattete Salons, Zimmer mit unverputztem Mauerwerk, dunklen Holzdecken und offenen Kaminen und sparsam möblierte Wintergärten, in denen nichts vom Blick in die Natur ablenkt. Kein Raum gleicht dem anderen, und jeder erzählt mit Details, die man oft erst nach Tagen entdeckt, seine eigene Geschichte. Den Zaubergarten von Santa Rita entdeckt man am besten zu Fuß oder im Pferdesattel und lässt sich abends bei Kerzenschein und Klassik mit argentinischen Menüs verwöhnen – alle Zutaten stammen soweit möglich aus eigenem Anbau.

Buchtipp: »Der Kuss der Spinnenfrau« von Manuel Puig

Bienvenue au royaume des fées

Le parc offre plus de tons de vert que ne pourrait en présenter la palette d'un peintre. Les arbres, les arbustes et la pelouse sont resplendissants dans leurs coloris vert foncé, vert clair, vert émeraude et vert tilleul. Avec ses quarante hectares la propriété est l'une des plus grandes Estancias de la région, et en tous cas la plus enchanteresse de toutes : au milieu de ce parc verdoyant trône le bâtiment principal de Santa Rita, un palais rose et crème aux ornements nombreux, avec ses arcs, ses colonnes et ses petites tours, un hommage à l'époque coloniale espagnole. C'est en 1790 que la famille Ezcurra fit construire les premiers bâtiments comme une sorte de ligne de défense tout autour de Buenos Aires. Plus tard Santa Rita fut remise à Antonio Carboni, le sénateur de la province, qui manifesta très clairement ses droits de propriétaire et fonda à quatre kilomètres de là le village de Carboni. Aujourd'hui la propriété appartient au couple Isabel Duggan et Franklin Nüdemberg ainsi qu'à leurs six filles, et est devenue depuis 1996 un hôtel enchanteur. Un mélange fantastique de styles règne à l'intérieur : chambres ornées de stuc, avec leurs étoffes artistement drapées et leurs lits à baldaquin, pièces aux murs sans crépi, avec leurs plafonds en bois sombre et leurs cheminées, jardins d'hiver meublés sobrement où rien ne vient détourner le regard de la nature. Aucune pièce ne ressemble à une autre et chacune nous conte sa propre histoire avec des détails que l'on ne remarque parfois qu'au bout de quelques jours. On ira à la découverte du parc enchanté à pied ou à cheval et le soir, à la lueur des chandelles, on savourera les menus argentins dont la plupart des produits proviennent de la propriété.

Livre à emporter : « Le baiser de la femme-araignée » de Manuel Puig

ANREISE	120 Kilometer südwestlich von Buenos Aires gelegen (90 Minuten Fahrtzeit)
PREISE	$
ZIMMER	9 Doppelzimmer
KÜCHE	Argentinische und internationale Spezialitäten; viele Zutaten aus eigenem Anbau
GESCHICHTE	1870 erbaut und seit 1996 ein kleines Hotel
X-FAKTOR	Schönster Stilmix mitten im Grünen

ACCÈS	Situé à 120 kilomètres au sud-ouest de Buenos Aires (90 minutes en voiture)
PRIX	$
CHAMBRES	9 chambres doubles
RESTAURATION	Spécialités argentines et internationales ; beaucoup de produits sont « maison »
HISTOIRE	Construit en 1870 et transformé en petit hôtel depuis 1996
LE « PETIT PLUS »	Le plus beau mélange de styles au milieu d'une nature verdoyante

Living like in olden times...
Hotel del Casco, Province Buenos Aires

Hotel del Casco,
Province Buenos Aires

Living like in olden times

This journey back into the past takes you a mere 24 kilometres (15 miles) from Buenos Aires. It leads to San Isidro
with its delightful historic centre – and the Hotel del Casco.
This former town house in the neo-classical style of the
19th century is on Avenida del Libertador and looks so absolutely spick and span you'd think they dusted it top to
bottom daily and polished every knob till it shone. With its
flight of marble steps, high windows, and slender pillars it
looks almost like a museum, keeping the charm of times
past sequestered from view. The quiet of the coolly-tiled
glass-roofed lobby, where ferns strike a note of colour under
the arches, prompts new arrivals to speak in undertones –
but it's a deference that's hardly necessary. Life is there to
be enjoyed at the Hotel del Casco, be it in the garden, on the
planted patio (the roof of which can be opened in fine weather), or in the rooms, their walls painted a Bordeaux red or
lime green or covered in subtly patterned papers. Antiques
of precious wood, crystal chandeliers, and free-standing bath-
tubs with claw feet create a classically stylish atmosphere –
knick-knacks of the sort beloved by so many Argentine hotel
proprietors will be sought here largely in vain. The note of
aristocratic grace is upheld in the vicinity. Opposite the hotel
is the Cathedral of San Isidro, the tower rising majestically
into the heavens, and there are walks to be taken in tranquil
gardens and parks or along the riverbank. And should this
idyllic world ever seem too peaceful, it's the easiest thing
to get back to the future: Buenos Aires is just 24 kilometres
(15 miles) away.

Book to pack: "Artificial Respiration" by Ricardo Piglia

Hotel del Casco
Avenida del Libertador 16.170
B1642CKV San Isidro Buenos Aires
Argentina
Tel. and Fax (54) 1147323993
E-mail: info@hoteldelcasco.com.ar
Website: www.hoteldelcasco.com.ar
www.great-escapes-hotels.com

DIRECTIONS	Situated 24 km/15 miles northeast of Buenos Aires, 45 km /28 miles from the international airport (50 minutes by road)
RATES	$$
ROOMS	12 double rooms, 2 apartments, 2 suites
FOOD	Classic Argentine cuisine
HISTORY	Located in a restored town residence built in 1892
X-FACTOR	Highly sophisticated

Wohnen wie in alten Zeiten

Die Reise von Buenos Aires zurück in die Vergangenheit ist nur 24 Kilometer lang. Sie führt nach San Isidro mit seinem hübschen historischen Zentrum – und mit dem Hotel del Casco. Die ehemalige Stadtresidenz im neoklassizistischen Stil des 19. Jahrhunderts steht an der Avenida del Libertador und sieht so rein und proper aus, als staubte man sie jeden Tag ab und polierte sie auf Hochglanz. Mit ihrer marmornen Freitreppe, den hohen Fenstern und schlanken Säulen wirkt sie fast wie ein Museum, das den Charme vergangener Zeiten birgt. Die Ruhe in der kühl gefliesten Lobby, in der Farne grüne Akzente setzen und über deren Bögen sich ein gläsernes Dach wölbt, lässt Neuankömmlinge unbewusst die Stimme senken – doch so viel Zurückhaltung ist gar nicht nötig. Im Hotel del Casco weiß man das Leben durchaus zu genießen, sei es im Garten, im bepflanzten Patio, dessen Dach bei schönem Wetter geöffnet werden kann, oder in den Zimmern, deren Wände in Bordeauxrot oder Lindgrün leuchten oder dezent gemusterte Tapeten besitzen. Antiquitäten aus wertvollem Holz, Kristallleuchter und frei stehende Badewannen mit geschwungenen Füßen sorgen für klassisch-elegantes Ambiente – Krimkrams und Nippes, den viele argentinische Hoteliers sonst so lieben, sucht man hier fast vergebens. Auf aristokratischen Pfaden wandeln kann man auch in der unmittelbaren Nachbarschaft: Gleich gegenüber dem Hotel steht die Kathedrale von San Isidro, deren Turm majestätisch in den Himmel ragt, und man spaziert durch ruhige Gärten und Parks oder am Flussufer entlang. Und sollte einem das Idyll doch einmal zu ruhig erscheinen, kommt man im Handumdrehen zurück in die Zukunft: Buenos Aires ist ja nur 24 Kilometer entfernt.

Buchtipp: »Künstliche Atmung« von Ricardo Piglia

Un voyage dans le passé

Pour voyager dans le passé, il suffit de se rendre à 24 kilomètres de Buenos Aires, dans le joli centre historique de San Isidro, et de résider à l'hôtel del Casco. L'ancien palais construit dans le style néo-classique du 19ᵉ siècle se trouve sur l'Avenida del Libertador et a l'air si resplendissant qu'on a l'impression qu'on lui enlève tous les jours sa poussière et qu'on le fait ensuite reluire avec un chiffon. Avec son escalier en marbre, ses hautes fenêtres et ses minces colonnes il ressemble presque à un musée qui abriterait tout le charme des époques passées. Le calme qui règne à la réception, recouverte d'un toit en verre et où les fougères ajoutent une petite note de vert, est si imposant que les nouveaux venus baissent directement le ton – mais une telle réserve n'est pas nécessaire. À l'hôtel del Casco on sait profiter de la vie, que ce soit dans le jardin, dans le patio verdoyant dont le toit peut être ouvert les jours de beau temps, ou dans les chambres aux murs rouge bordeaux et vert tilleul et dont le sol est recouvert de tapis aux motifs décents. Les antiquités en bois précieux, les lustres en cristal et les baignoires aux pieds recourbés procurent une ambiance classique et élégante, et l'on cherchera en vain toutes ces babioles que les hôteliers argentins aiment tant. Dehors on restera dans cette même ambiance puisqu'en face de l'hôtel se trouve la cathédrale de San Isidro, dont la tour s'élève majestueusement dans le ciel, et l'on se promènera dans les parcs et jardins tranquilles ou le long de la rivière. Et si cette atmosphère idyllique nous semble un peu trop calme, on se retrouvera en un rien de temps à notre époque moderne, car Buenos Aires n'est qu'à 24 kilomètres de là.

Livre à emporter : « Respiration artificielle » de Ricardo Piglia

ANREISE	24 Kilometer nordöstlich von Buenos Aires gelegen, 45 Kilometer vom Internationalen Flughafen entfernt (50 Min. Fahrtzeit)
PREISE	$$
ZIMMER	12 Doppelzimmer, 2 Apartments, 2 Suiten
KÜCHE	Klassische argentinische Küche
GESCHICHTE	In einem restaurierten Stadtpalais aus dem Jahr 1892 untergebracht
X-FAKTOR	Sehr sophisticated

ACCÈS	Situé à 24 kilomètres au nord-est de Buenos Aires, à 45 kilomètres de l'aéroport (50 min. en voiture)
PRIX	$$
CHAMBRES	12 chambres doubles, 2 appartements, 2 suites
RESTAURATION	Cuisine argentine classique
HISTOIRE	Palais restauré en 1892
LE « PETIT PLUS »	Très sophistiqué

Life in the sun...
Ten Rivers & Ten Lakes Lodge, Patagonia

Ten Rivers Lodge, Patagonia

Life in the sun

It was love at first sight. When young British actress Renée Dickinson went to Patagonia in the Thirties, she found her personal place to be. She had a lodge built of cypress wood in the densely forested hills of the Lanín National Park, with a view of Lago Lacar and the Andes that was lovelier by far than any theatre backdrop. She called the house "Arrayán", which means, in the language of the Mapuche, "The place where the rays of the setting sun fall". But Dickinson was to enjoy that sunlight for just four years. In 1943 she fell ill whilst travelling, and died in Buenos Aires, aged only 31. After her death, her brother Barney and his family took over the property and transformed it into one of the finest hotels in the country, the Ten Rivers Lodge. Celebrities and diplomats from all around the world have vacationed here and have enjoyed the fly-fishing – for the rivers and lakes of Patagonia are a true El Dorado of trout and salmon. If fishing isn't quite for you, the rugged and uncannily beautiful landscape is there to be discovered, on foot or on horseback, climbing or mountainbiking. Visit the mountain town of San Martín de los Andes, or go birdwatching. And whatever you choose to do with your day, in the evenings the Lodge coddles you with cosy luxury (cypress remains the dominant note) and culinary treats. The wine cellar can satisfy even the most demanding of sommeliers, and the cuisine wonderfully marries South American and Mediterranean fragrances and flavours – the lamb of Patagonia is legendary.

Book to pack: "Asleep in the sun" by Adolfo Bioy Casares

Ten Rivers Lodge
Circuito km 4.5
San Martín de los Andes
Neuquén
Argentina
Tel. (54) 59177710, -11, -16
Fax (54) 1141154000, int. 118
E-mail: info@tenriverstenlakes.com
Website: www.tenriverstenlakes.com
www.great-escapes-hotels.com

DIRECTIONS	Located near San Martín de los Andes, a 20-minute drive from Chapelco airport (domestic flights from Buenos Aires). Transfer is organised
RATES	$$
ROOMS	3 double rooms, 1 apartment for 3 people (with living room and open fireplace)
FOOD	The restaurant serves South American and Mediterranean cuisine (with an emphasis on lamb and game)
HISTORY	An actress's dream house turned into a luxury lodge
X-FACTOR	Active vacation and relaxation

Sonnige Zeiten

Es war Liebe auf den ersten Blick. Als die junge britische Schauspielerin Renée Dickinson in den dreißiger Jahren nach Patagonien kam, fand sie ihren persönlichen *place to be*: In den dicht bewaldeten Hügeln des Lanín-Nationalparks ließ sie sich eine Lodge bauen; ganz aus Zypressenholz und mit einem Blick auf den Lago Lacar und die Anden, der schöner als jede Theaterkulisse war. Sie nannte das Haus »Arrayán«, was in der Sprache der Mapuche so viel bedeutet wie »Der Ort, auf den die Strahlen der untergehenden Sonne fallen« – doch sie durfte dieses Leuchten gerade einmal vier Jahre genießen. 1943 erkrankte sie während einer Reise und starb in Buenos Aires; nur 31 Jahre alt. Nach ihrem Tod übernahmen ihr Bruder Barney und seine Familie das Anwesen und verwandelten es in eine der schönsten Adressen des Landes, in die Ten Rivers Lodge. Berühmtheiten und Botschafter aus aller Welt verbrachten hier bereits ihren Urlaub und versuchten sich im Fliegenfischen – denn die Flüsse und Seen Patagoniens sind ein Eldorado für Forellen und Lachse. Wer sich mit dem nassen Element nicht anfreunden kann, entdeckt die raue und fast unwirklich schöne Landschaft beim Wandern und Reiten, Klettern und Mountainbiken, besichtigt das Gebirgsstädtchen San Martín de los Andes oder geht zum Birdwatching. Ganz egal, für welches Tagesprogramm man sich entscheidet: Abends verwöhnt die Lodge mit warmem Luxus (Zypressenholz ist noch immer das dominierende Element) und kulinarischen Festen: Der Weinkeller genügt selbst Ansprüchen großer Sommeliers, und die Küche verbindet südamerikanische und mediterrane Aromen – vor allem das patagonische Lamm ist legendär.

Buchtipp: »Schlaf in der Sonne« von Adolfo Bioy Casares

Les rayons du soleil couchant

Ce fut un vrai coup de foudre. Lorsque la jeune actrice britannique Renée Dickinson arriva en Patagonie dans les années 1930, elle sut tout de suite qu'elle allait y rester et se fit construire un lodge dans les collines boisées du parc national de Lanín. Sa maison en bois de cyprès offrait une vue incomparable sur le Lago Lacar et sur les Andes. La jeune femme la baptisa « Arrayán », ce qui signifie dans le dialecte des Mapuche « le lieu sur lequel tombent les rayons du soleil couchant ». Malheureusement, elle ne profita de cette lumière que quatre ans. Elle tomba malade lors d'un voyage en 1943 et mourut à Buenos Aires ; elle était âgée de 31 ans seulement. Après sa mort, son frère Barney et sa famille reprirent la maison et la transformèrent en l'une des plus belles adresses du pays, le Ten Rivers Lodge. Des personalités et des ambassadeurs du monde entier y ont passé leurs vacances et se sont essayé à la pêche au lancer. Il faut dire aussi que les rivières et les lacs de Patagonie sont un El Dorado pour pêcheurs et regorgent de truites et de saumons. Si l'on n'aime pas trop se mouiller les pieds, on peut partir à la découverte de cette région rude et presque irréelle : à pied, à cheval, en faisant de l'escalade ou du V. T. T. On visitera aussi la petite ville montagneuse de San Martín de los Andes ou on partira observer les oiseaux. Quel que soit le programme de la journée, une chose est sûre : le soir, le lodge vous chouchoutera avec son luxe cosy (le bois de cyprès est encore l'élément dominant) et ses fêtes culinaires. La cave des vins satisfait les sommeliers les plus exigeants et la cuisine allie les arômes sud-américains et méditerranéens – en particulier l'agneau de Patagonie est légendaire.

Livre à emporter : « La trame céleste » de Adolfo Bioy Casares

ANREISE	Bei San Martín de los Andes gelegen, 20 Fahrtminuten vom Flughafen Chapelco entfernt (dorthin Inlandsflüge ab Buenos Aires). Transfer wird organisiert	ACCÈS	Situé près de San Martín de los Andes, à 20 minutes en voiture de l'aéroport de Chapelco (vols intérieurs depuis Buenos Aires). Le transfert est organisé
PREISE	$$	PRIX	$$
ZIMMER	3 Doppelzimmer, 1 Apartment für 3 Personen (mit Wohnzimmer und offenem Kamin)	CHAMBRES	3 chambres doubles, 1 studio pour 3 personnes (avec salle de séjour et cheminée)
KÜCHE	Restaurant mit südamerikanischen und mediterranen Menüs (viel Lamm und Wild)	RESTAURATION	Restaurant proposant des menus sud-américains et méditerranéens (en particulier agneau et gibier)
GESCHICHTE	Das Traumhaus einer Schauspielerin wurde zur luxuriösen Lodge	HISTOIRE	La maison de rêve d'une actrice a été transformée en lodge luxurieux
X-FAKTOR	Aktivurlaub und Ausspannen	LE « PETIT PLUS »	Vacances actives et détente

A farmstead by a river...
Estancia Arroyo Verde, Patagonia

A farmstead by a river

The sparkling blue waters are crystal clear, and as it flows majestically through the valley it is brimful of salmon and trout – the Traful is every fly-fisher's dream. In the Nahuel Huapi National Park in northern Patagonia, where millions of years ago the earth was invisible beneath vast glaciers, the season opens on the second Saturday in November and runs till the third Sunday in April. Throughout those months the anglers are to be seen in their waders standing in the river, making their skilful (or in some cases not so skilful) casts and waiting patiently for the next bite. Most days the fish will weigh in at three to four pounds, and on a good day a ten-pounder will be reeled in from the Traful. If you like spending your time in the right kind of setting, among others who share your interests, book in to the Estancia Arroyo Verde and get a taste of Argentine country living at its best. Cattle and sheep graze the pastures at the foot of an impressive massif, and the stone and timber farmhouse itself is furnished in the South American country manner with deep armchairs, hunting trophies and knick-knacks. In the evenings, eat with silver cutlery off antique china, or barbecue down by the river if the weather's warm. For those who aren't here for the fishing alone, Arroyo Verde also offers riding and trekking in the Andes, or birdwatching in the land of the condor.

Book to pack: "Around the day in 80 worlds" by Julio Cortázar

Estancia Arroyo Verde
c/o Meme Larivière
Billinghurst 2586, 3° Piso
Buenos Aires
Argentina
Tel. and Fax (54) 1148017448
E-mail: info@estanciaarroyoverde.com.ar
Website: www.estanciaarroyoverde.com.ar
www.great-escapes-hotels.com

DIRECTIONS	Situated 67 km/41 miles southeast of Bariloche airport
RATES	$$$$
ROOMS	4 double rooms in the main building, 1 lakeside chalet for 2 to 4
FOOD	Home cooking; the picnics and barbecue evenings
HISTORY	A ranch was transformed into an adventure playground for those seeking an active holiday
X-FACTOR	One of South America's prime locations for fly-fishing

Die Farm am Fluss

Sein blau glitzerndes Wasser ist kristallklar, er fließt majestätisch durchs Tal und bringt ganze Schwärme von Lachsen und Forellen mit sich – der Traful ist der Traum aller Fliegenfischer. Im Norden Patagoniens, wo vor Millionen von Jahren riesige Gletscher die Erde bedeckten und sich heute der Nationalpark Nahuel Huapi ausdehnt, beginnt die Saison am zweiten Samstag im November und dauert bis zum dritten Sonntag im April. Dann stehen die Angler in hohen Gummistiefeln im Wasser, werfen mit (mehr oder weniger) wohl geübten Bewegungen ihre langen Leinen aus und warten geduldig auf den nächsten Fang – drei bis vier Pfund bringen die Fische an normalen Tagen auf die Waage, an Glückstagen kann man aber durchaus auch einen satten Zehnpfünder aus den Fluten ziehen. Wer standesgemäß und unter Gleichgesinnten wohnen möchte, reserviert am besten in der Estancia Arroyo Verde und erlebt dort das argentinische Landleben *at its best*. Auf den Weiden am Fuß eines beeindruckenden Felsmassivs werden Rinder und Schafe gezüchtet, das Farmhaus aus Stein und Holz ist im südamerikanischen Countrystil mit viel Nippes, Jagdtrophäen sowie tiefen Sesseln zum Versinken eingerichtet, und man isst abends mit Silberbesteck von antikem Porzellan oder grillt bei warmem Wetter am Flussufer. Für alle, die ihre Tage nicht nur mit den Fischen verbringen wollen, bietet Arroyo Verde auch Ausritte und Trekkingtouren in den Anden an oder schickt sie zum Birdwatching auf den Spuren des Condors.

Buchtipp: »Reise um den Tag in 80 Welten« von Julio Cortázar

Le ranch au bord du fleuve

Il coule majestueusement à travers la vallée, ses eaux sont d'une pureté cristalline et elles regorgent de saumons et de truites. Le Traful est bien le paradis des pêcheurs. Dans le nord de la Patagonie, là où s'étendaient d'énormes glaciers il y a plusieurs millions d'années et où se trouve aujourd'hui le parc national de Nahuel Huapi, la saison de la pêche au lancer commence le deuxième samedi du mois de novembre pour se terminer le troisième dimanche du mois d'avril. Pendant cette période, les pêcheurs qui ont enfilé leurs cuissardes lancent leur ligne avec plus ou moins d'adresse et attendent patiemment que le poisson morde. En général, les poissons qu'ils attrapent pèsent entre trois et quatre livres, ce qui n'est pas négligeable, mais les jours de chance ils peuvent aussi avoir une belle prise qui pèsera ses dix livres sur la balance. Celui qui désire résider dans un hôtel de qualité parmi des gens qui partagent ses goûts, sera bien avisé de réserver une chambre à l'Estancia Arroyo Verde où il pourra aussi découvrir la vie à la campagne sous son meilleur côté. Des élevages de bœufs et de moutons paissent tranquillement dans les prairies au pied d'une formation rocheuse impressionnante. Le ranch, construit en pierre et en bois, présente un style campagnard sud-américain, avec beaucoup de bibelots, de trophées de chasse et de fauteuils dont la mollesse et la profondeur invitent au repos. Le soir, on sort l'argenterie et la porcelaine ou, quand le temps s'y prête, on organise un barbecue sur la rive du fleuve. Pour ceux qui ne désirent pas s'adonner à la pêche toute la journée, Arroyo Verde propose aussi des randonnées à pied ou à cheval dans les Andes ainsi que la possibilité de partir sur les traces du condor.

Livre à emporter : « Le tour du jour en 80 mondes » de Julio Cortázar

ANREISE	67 Kilometer südöstlich des Flughafens Bariloche
PREISE	$$$$
ZIMMER	4 Doppelzimmer im Haupthaus, 1 Chalet am See für 2 bis 4 Personen
KÜCHE	Hausmannskost; Picknicks und Grillabende
GESCHICHTE	Aus einer Ranch wurde ein Abenteuerspielplatz für Aktivurlauber
X-FAKTOR	Einer der besten Plätze fürs Fliegenfischen in Südamerika

ACCÈS	67 kilomètres au sud-est de l'aéroport de Bariloche
PRIX	$$$$
CHAMBRES	4 chambres doubles dans le bâtiment principal, 1 chalet au bord du lac pour 2 à 4 personnes
RESTAURATION	Cuisine maison ; pique-niques et soirées barbecue
HISTOIRE	Un ranch s'est transformé en terrain d'aventure pour touristes désirant des vacances actives
LE « PETIT PLUS »	L'un des meilleurs endroits pour la pêche au lancer dans toute l'Amérique du Sud

Close to the Ice Age...
Los Notros, Patagonia

Close to the Ice Age

The masses of ice glint a whitish-blue by day, and at evening glow orange. As if in slow motion they grind their way through the mountains, and tumble with a mighty roar into the waters of the Canal de los Témpanos. To stand before the Perito Moreno is to feel transported to some unreal science fiction scenario – and to experience one of the most arresting natural spectacles on earth. The Perito Moreno is the most famous of the 47 glaciers in Argentina's Los Glaciares National Park. It is a giant, soaring up to 60 metres (197 feet) out of the water, the surface as soft as frozen meringue and as pointed as billions of icy needles. If you prefer not to venture right up close, either by ship or on a trekking expedition, you can admire the glacier from a distance – for preference, from the terrace of the Los Notros Hotel. Viviana and Michel Biquard discovered the unique plot on the tip of the Magellan Peninsula in the late Eighties and built a house like a box in a theatre. Panoramic windows are the key feature even in the bathrooms. Not that that's the only way you're uniquely spoilt at Los Notros. Every one of the 32 rooms is differently furnished, with deep wing armchairs and iron bedsteads, hand-woven carpets and antique pictures. There is a cosy library where amateur students of glaciers will find all they wish to know about the Perito Moreno. There's a cigar lounge and a restaurant serving Argentine beef but also lamb, game, and fish. The herbs and spices are from the hotel's own garden, as are the desserts – the crème brûlée with a hint of lavender is surpassed only by the view of the glacier.

Book to pack: "The Old Patagonian" by Paul Theroux

Los Notros	
Facing the Perito Moreno Glacier	
Santa Cruz	
Argentina	
Tel. (54) 2902499510 and -11	
Fax (54) 1152778222	
E-mail: info@experiencepatagonia.com	
Website: www.losnotros.com	
www.great-escapes-hotels.com	

DIRECTIONS	Situated 30 km/20 miles east of El Calafate airport. Transfer is organised
RATES	$$$$
ROOMS	12 Cascade double rooms, 8 Superior doubles, 12 Premium doubles
FOOD	The regional specialities of Patagonia and Argentine wines
HISTORY	The only building on the tip of the Magellan Peninsula, built in the late 1980s
X-FACTOR	The might of the glaciers on your doorstep

Der Eiszeit so nah

Seine Eismassen glitzern tagsüber in Weiß-blau und glühen abends in Orange, sie schieben sich wie in Zeitlupe knirschend durch die Berge und stürzen von mächtigem Donner begleitet in die Fluten des Canal de los Témpanos – wer vor dem Perito Moreno steht, fühlt sich wie in einer irrealen Sciencefiction-Szene und erlebt doch eines der faszinierendsten Naturschauspiele der Erde. Der Perito Moreno ist der berühmteste von 47 Gletschern im argentinischen Nationalpark Los Glaciares; ein Gigant, dessen Oberfläche gleichzeitig so sanft wie gefrorenes Baiser und so spitz wie Milliarden eisiger Nadeln aussieht. Wer dem bis zu 60 Meter aus dem Wasser ragenden Gletscher nicht gleich per Schiff oder beim Trekking näher kommen möchte, kann ihn auch erst aus einiger Entfernung bewundern – am besten von der Terrasse des Hotels Los Notros aus. Viviana und Michel Biquard haben das einzigartige Grundstück an der Spitze der Magallanes-Halbinsel Ende der 80er Jahre entdeckt und hier ein Haus wie eine Theaterloge gebaut. Panoramafenster sind selbst in den Bädern das wichtigste Gestaltungselement, doch auch sonst verzichtet Los Notros nicht auf einmalige Erlebnisse. Jedes der 32 Zimmer ist unterschiedlich eingerichtet, mit tiefen Ohrensesseln und Eisenbetten, handgewebten Teppichen und antiken Bildern. Es gibt eine gemütliche Bibliothek, in der Hobby-Glaciologen alles über den Perito Moreno finden, eine Zigarrenlounge und ein Restaurant, in dem argentinisches Rindfleisch ebenso auf der Karte steht wie Lamm, Wild und Fisch. Verfeinert wird jedes Gericht mit Kräutern und Gewürzen aus dem eigenen Garten – das gilt sogar für die Nachspeisen: Die Crème brûlée mit einem Hauch Lavendel wird nur noch von der Aussicht auf den Gletscher übertroffen.

Buchtipp: »Im Feuerland« von Eduardo Belgrano Rawson

Se retrouver à l'ère glacière

Ses blocs de glace jettent dans la journée des lueurs bleutées et s'enflamment le soir dans des tons orangés, ils se poussent doucement les uns les autres en craquant, puis s'effondrent dans un effroyable bruit de tonnerre dans les eaux du Canal de los Témpanos – quand on se trouve devant le Perito Moreno, on a l'impression de voir une scène de science-fiction face au fascinant spectacle qu'il nous offre. Le Perito Moreno est le plus célèbre des 47 glaciers du parc national argentin de Los Glaciares. Il est un géant dont l'extérieur semble aussi moelleux qu'une meringue et aussi acéré que des milliards d'épines glacées. Celui qui ne désire pas se rapprocher en bateau ou en faisant du trekking de ce géant de 60 mètres, peut aussi le contempler de loin. Le mieux est encore de le faire de la terrasse de l'hôtel Los Notros. Après avoir découvert, dans les années 1980, ce terrain exceptionnel de la presqu'île de Magallanes, Viviana et Michel Biquard y ont construit une maison qui évoque une loge de théâtre. Même dans les salles de bains, les fenêtres panoramiques sont l'élément dominant bien que Los Nostros ne renonce pas à une décoration hors pair. Chacune des 32 chambres est aménagée de façon différente, avec de confortables bergères, des lits en fer, des tapis tissés à la main et des photos anciennes. Il y a une bibliothèque dans laquelle les amoureux des glaciers trouveront tous les renseignements sur le Perito Moreno, un fumoir et un restaurant qui propose au menu du bœuf argentin, de l'agneau, du gibier et du poisson. Chaque plat reçoit une saveur incomparable grâce aux fines herbes et aux épices du jardin et cela vaut aussi pour les desserts : la crème brûlée aromatisée à la lavande est un délice que seul la vue sur le glacier est capable de surpasser.

Livre à emporter : « Le naufragé des étoiles » de Eduardo Belgrano Rawson

ANREISE	30 Kilometer östlich des Flughafens El Calafate gelegen. Transfer wird organisiert	ACCÈS	Situé à 30 kilomètres à l'est de l'aéroport d'El Calafate. Le transfert est organisé
PREISE	$$$$	PRIX	$$$$
ZIMMER	12 Doppelzimmer Cascade, 8 Doppelzimmer Superior, 12 Doppelzimmer Premium	CHAMBRES	12 chambres doubles Cascade, 8 chambres doubles Superior, 12 chambres doubles Premium
KÜCHE	Regionale Spezialitäten aus Patagonien und argentinische Weine	RESTAURATION	Spécialités de Patagonie, bœuf et vins argentins
GESCHICHTE	Ende der 80er Jahre als einziges Gebäude an der Spitze der Magallanes-Halbinsel erbaut	HISTOIRE	Construit à la fin des années 1980. Seul bâtiment à la pointe de la presqu'île de Magallanes
X-FAKTOR	Gletschergewalten direkt vor der Tür	LE « PETIT PLUS »	Le spectacle grandiose du glacier devant la porte

Patagonia and nothing but...
explora en Patagonia, Patagonia

Patagonia and nothing but

It is the end of the world. A raw, rugged landscape where once colonial powers competed for the upper hand, and whalers and sealers made a living out of their bloody pursuit. But it is also country of almost unreal beauty: Patagonia, in southern Chile. Rarely will your loungs breathe so bracing an air. Rarely will you see such emerald-green lakes or such breathtaking mountain chains. In the very heart of the region is the Torres del Paine National Park, a region of granite needles, glacial waters, forests, and vast mosses, which is under UNESCO protection. It was there that explora Hotels opened their first establishment in 1993, the explora en Patagonia, which looks very much as if it were an immense liner lying at anchor on the shoreline of Lago Pehoé. Chilean designer Germán de Sol has cast the architecture in an entirely marine mould, with a wood-cladding façade, a landing stage, a reception area resembling a canin, and model ships in the lobby. As on a ship's deck, the rooms lie along seemingly endless passageways, and are fitted out in natural materials such as wood, hides, or stone. The philosophy of the house calls for purist quality, as evidenced in accessories such as hand-woven bed linen, rough-cut cakes of soap in the bathroom, or an entire ham on the breakfast buffet – it is an experience that involves all the senses and affords the purest encounter with nature. This is also true of the bath-house with its panoramic view of the lake and mountains, and of the expeditions on offer every day – when professional guides lead visitors into the secret heart of Patagonia.

Book to pack: "In Patagonia" by Bruce Chatwin

explora en Patagonia
Hotel Salto Chico S/N, Comuna Torres
del Paine
Casilia 57, Puerto Natales
Patagonia, Chile
Tel. (56) 2 2066060
Fax (56) 2 2284655
Website: www.explora.com
www.great-escapes-hotels.com

DIRECTIONS	Situated 200 km/125 miles northwest of Punta Arenas (domestic flights from Santiago). Transfer by minibus is organised
RATES	$$$
ROOMS	26 Cordillera Paine double rooms, 4 Exploradores suites
FOOD	First-rate, purist cuisine using fresh fish, vegetables, and fruit. There is also a bar
HISTORY	Opened in October 1993
X-FACTOR	Discover the end of the world!

Patagonien pur

Es ist das Ende der Welt; eine raue Landschaft, in der einst Kolonialmächte um die Vorherrschaft stritten und Wal- und Robbenjäger mit blutigen Methoden um ihren Lebensunterhalt kämpften – doch es ist auch eine Landschaft von fast unwirklicher Schönheit: Patagonien im Süden Chiles. Selten atmet man eine so kristallklare Luft wie hier, blickt auf smaragdgrün schimmernde Seen und auf Bergketten wie überdimensionale Fototapeten. Im Herzen dieser Region liegt der Nationalpark Torres del Paine, von der Unesco geschützt und geprägt von Granitnadeln, Gletscherwasser, Wäldern sowie Moosflächen. Hier haben die explora-Hotels 1993 ihr erstes Haus eröffnet: das explora en Patagonia, das wie ein riesiger Dampfer am Ufer des Lago Pehoé vor Anker zu liegen scheint. Der chilenische Designer Germán de Sol setzt ganz auf eine bootartige Architektur – mit einer holzverkleideten Fassade, einem Zutrittssteg, einer kajütenähnlichen Rezeption und Schiffsmodellen in der Halle. Wie auf einem Deck liegen die Zimmer entlang scheinbar endloser Flure und sind mit natürlichen Materialien wie Holz, Fell oder Stein eingerichtet. Dass die Philosophie des Hauses der edle Purismus ist, merkt man an Accessoires wie handgewebter Bettwäsche, groben Seifestücken im Bad oder einem ganzen Schinken auf dem Frühstücksbuffet – hier soll man alle Sinne einsetzen und die Natur in ihrer reinsten Form erleben. Das gilt auch für Besuche im Badehaus mit Panoramablick auf See und Berge sowie für die Expeditionen, die jeden Tag angeboten werden – geführt von professionellen Guides kommen die Gäste so den Geheimnissen Patagoniens auf die Spur.

Buchtipp: »In Patagonien« von Bruce Chatwin

Purisme en Patagonie

La Patagonie, c'est au bout du monde, une terre sauvage qui a vu les luttes d'influence entre les puissances coloniales et les chasseurs de baleines et de phoques se battre pour survivre dans un environnement aussi rude qu'eux. Mais sa beauté est presque irréelle. L'air y est d'une pureté cristalline, les lacs chatoient, couleur d'émeraude, au pied de la cordillère spectaculaire. C'est au cœur de cette région que se trouve le parc national Torres del Paine, protégé par l'Unesco, avec ses tours granitiques, ses glaciers, ses chutes d'eau, ses forêts et sa steppe. En 1993, la chaîne explora-Hotels a ouvert ici son premier hôtel, l'explora en patagonia, qui semble amarré, tel un gigantesque vapeur, sur les rives du Lago Pehoé.

Le designer chilien Germán de Sol a misé sur une architecture navale – façade habillée de bois, passerelle, « cabine » de réception – et décoré le hall de maquettes de bateau. Les chambres, disposées comme sur un pont dans de longs corridors, sont décorées de matériaux naturels comme le bois, la fourrure ou la pierre.

L'ambiance est imprégnée de purisme, on le remarque par exemple dans la literie tissée à la main, les morceaux de savon « grossiers » dans la salle de bains ou le jambon entier que propose le buffet du petit-déjeuner. Ici, tous les sens doivent entrer en action et percevoir la nature dans sa forme la plus pure. Le même souci de noble simplicité règne dans la maison de bains qui offre un panorama splendide sur le lac et les montagnes ainsi que sur les expéditions proposées tous les jours. Accompagnés par des guides professionnels, les hôtes s'en vont percer les mystères de la Patagonie.

Livre à emporter : « En Patagonie » de Bruce Chatwin

ANREISE	200 Kilometer nordwestlich von Punta Arenas gelegen (dorthin Inlandsflüge ab Santiago), Transfer im Minibus wird organisiert
PREISE	$$$
ZIMMER	26 Doppelzimmer Cordillera Paine, 4 Suiten Exploradores
KÜCHE	Erstklassig und ebenfalls dem Purismus verpflichtet – mit frischem Fisch, Gemüse und Obst. Außerdem eine Bar
GESCHICHTE	Im Oktober 1993 eröffnet
X-FAKTOR	Entdecken Sie das Ende der Welt!

ACCÈS	Situé à 200 kilomètres au nord-ouest de Punta Arenas (là-bas, vols intérieurs à partir de Santiago), un transfert en minibus est organisé
PRIX	$$$
CHAMBRES	26 chambres doubles Cordillera Paine, 4 suites Exploradores
RESTAURATION	De premier choix, avec également des accents puristes – poisson frais, légumes et fruits. Et un bar
HISTOIRE	Ouvert en octobre 1993
LE « PETIT PLUS »	Pour découvrir le bout du monde !

A question of style...
Hotel Antumalal, Araucanía

A question of style

In October 1938 a young couple fleeing the impending Second World War, Guillermo and Catalina Pollak from Prague, arrived in Pucón with dreams of making a new life for themselves in Chile. But at first their chosen home at the other side of the world proved full of obstacles. A volcanic eruption and a fire destroyed the Pollakstet club and hotel. Ten years later, however, all was well and things were on the up at last – literally so. High on a rocky plateau above Lake Villarrica, together with Chilean architect Jorge Elton, the couple created what has remained to this day one of the most unusual hotels in all South America: a long, flat building in the Bauhaus style. Antumalal ("sunshine court" in the language of the Mapuche people) commands views across a garden of flowers, far across the water, to the volcano, the snow-capped summit of which looks as if it had been powdered with icing sugar. No wonder the rooms don't trouble with such profane distractions as televisions – the view from the panoramic windows is far better than any movie. The design focusses on native wood and Chilean country style; every room has its own fireplace as standard. An entertaining mixture of Czech and South American dishes is served in the restaurant, and the proprietors are especially proud of their bar counter, which measures 3.99 metres (about 13 feet) and was fashioned from a single piece of timber. The splendid Chilean wines should not be over-indulged in, though – it would be a pity to spoil your delight in nearby Huerquehue National Park by visiting with a hang-over!

Book to pack: "Memoirs" by Pablo Neruda

Hotel Antumalal	
Casilia 84	
Pucón	
Chile	
Tel. (56) 45 441011 and -12	
Fax (56) 45 441013	
E-mail: info@antumalal.com	
Website: www.antumalal.com	
www.great-escapes-hotels.com	

DIRECTIONS	Situated 125 km/80 miles southeast of Temuco airport, which is reached by domestic flight from Santiago. 90-minute transfer to hotel on request
RATES	$
ROOMS	11 double rooms, 1 suite, 1 family suite, 1 Royal Chalet
FOOD	"Restaurant del Parque" serving Czech-Chilean cuisine. Also, "Don Guillermo's Bar"
HISTORY	Opened in 1950, the hotel was built in the Bauhaus style
X-FACTOR	Unique architecture, unique views

Eine Frage des Stils

Es war im Oktober 1938, als Guillermo und Catalina Pollak
aus Prag nach Pucón kamen – ein junges Ehepaar auf der
Flucht vor dem Zweiten Weltkrieg und voller Träume von
einem neuen Leben in Chile. Doch die Wahlheimat am
anderen Ende der Welt lag anfangs voller Stolpersteine: Ein
Vulkanausbruch und ein Feuer zerstörten den Club und das
Hotel, das die Pollaks betrieben. Aber nach zehn Jahren ging
es endlich aufwärts – im wahrsten Sinne des Wortes: Auf
einem Felsplateau hoch über dem Villarrica-See entwarfen
die beiden gemeinsam mit dem chilenischen Architekten
Jorge Elton eines der damals wie heute ungewöhnlichsten
Hotels in Südamerika: ein flaches, lang gezogenes Gebäude
im Bauhausstil. Antumalal (»Sonnenhof« in der Sprache der
Mapuche) blickt auf einen blühenden Garten, weit über das
Wasser und bis zum Vulkan, dessen schneebedeckte Kuppe
wie mit Puderzucker bestreut wirkt. Kein Wunder, dass
die Zimmer auf so profane Dinge wie einen Fernseher verzichten – die Sicht aus den Panoramafenstern schlägt
jeden Blockbuster. Das Design konzentriert sich auf einhei-
misches Holz und chilenischen Countrystil; ein eigener
Kamin gehört in jedem Raum zum Standard. Eine amüsante
Mischung aus tschechischen und südamerikanischen
Gerichten wird im Restaurant serviert, und besonders stolz
sind die Inhaber auf ihren Bartresen, der 3,99 Meter lang ist
und aus einem einzigen Holzstück geschliffen wurde. Zu
viel chilenischen Wein sollte man hier allerdings nicht
bestellen – mit Kopfschmerzen wären die Exkursionen in
den nahen Huerquehue National Park nur halb so ein-
drucksvoll.
Buchtipp: »Ich bekenne, ich habe gelebt« von Pablo Neruda

Question de style

Guillermo et Catalina Pollak se revoient en octobre 1938,
jeune couple fuyant Prague et la Deuxième Guerre mondiale avec le rêve d'une vie meilleure à Pucón au Chili.
Néanmoins, ce pays du bout du monde leur réservait aussi
d'autres écueils, d'ordre naturel cette fois : le club et l'hôtel
qu'ils exploitaient au début ont été détruits par une éruption
volcanique et un incendie. Enfin, au bout de dix ans, ils ont
vu leurs efforts récompensés. Sur un plateau rocheux au-
dessus du lac Villarrica, Guillermo et Catalina Pollak ont
conçu en collaboration avec l'architecte chilien Jorge Elton
ce qui est resté à ce jour l'un des hôtels les plus insolites
d'Amérique latine et se présente comme une construction
longue et basse de style Bauhaus.
Antumalal (« cour du soleil » en mapuche) se dresse au-
dessus d'un jardin fleuri, il surplombe la mer et regarde au
loin le volcan dont la cime enneigée à l'air saupoudrée de
sucre glace. Les chambres se passent de choses aussi pro-
fanes qu'un téléviseur – on délaisserait le meilleur film à
succès pour le panorama qui s'ouvre à la fenêtre. Le design
est concentré sur les essences locales et le style rustique
chilien ; chaque chambre possède une cheminée.
La cuisine servie ici est un mélange amusant de spécialités
tchèques et sud-américaines, et les propriétaires sont parti-
culièrement fiers de leur bar de 3,99 mètres taillé dans un
seul tronc d'arbre. Toutefois, attention à la migraine, celui
qui veut partir frais et dispos en excursion au Huerquehue
National Park tout proche veillera à consommer les vins
chiliens avec modération.
Livre à emporter : « J'avoue que j'ai vécu » de Pablo Neruda

ANREISE	125 Kilometer südöstlich des Flughafens Temuco gelegen (dorthin Inlandsflüge ab Santiago. 90-minütiger Transfer zum Hotel auf Wunsch)
PREISE	$
ZIMMER	11 Doppelzimmer, 1 Suite, 1 Family Suite, 1 Royal Chalet
KÜCHE	»Restaurant del Parque« mit tschechisch-chilenischer Küche. Außerdem »Don Guillermo's Bar«
GESCHICHTE	1950 eröffnet, im Bauhausstil erbaut
X-FAKTOR	Einzigartige Architektur, einzigartige Aussicht

ACCÈS	Situé à 125 kilomètres au sud-est de l'aéroport de Temuco (vols intérieurs à partir de Santiago). Transfert de 90 minutes sur demande
PRIX	$
CHAMBRES	11 doubles, 1 suite, 1 Family Suite, 1 Royal Chalet
RESTAURATION	Cuisine tchéco-chilienne au « Restaurant del Parque ». Et puis « Don Guillermo's Bar »
HISTOIRE	Construction de style Bauhaus, ouvert en 1950
LE « PETIT PLUS »	Architecture unique, panorama unique

A summer residence in the s

Hotel Casa Real, Región Metropolitana

uth...

Hotel Casa Real,
Región Metropolitana

A summer residence in the south

When Domingo Fernández Concha established the Santa
Rita winery in 1880, his aim for the future was not only to
grow some of Chile's best wines – he also wanted to live in
one of the nation's finest houses. So he had a luxury country
residence built south of Santiago, in the Pompeian style,
with majestic flights of steps, slender pillars, and high windows. He resided beneath richly ornamented wooden ceilings and crystal chandeliers, viewed his reflection in gilt-
framed mirrors, and hung gleaming oil paintings on his
walls. He even had a billiards table imported from Great
Britain. And all of this grand style can be savoured to this
day; for in 1996 the house became the Hotel Casa Real,
offering guests a veritable journey into the past. Indeed,
the grounds laid out in 1882 by French landscape architect
Guillermo Renner may well be even finer than they originally were, having matured into an enchanting estate with cen-
tury-old cedars, almond, olive, and lemon trees, and what
may well be the largest bougainvillea on the entire continent. The hotel also has the Doña Paula Restaurant, named
after the former owner, and an homage to Chile's indepen-
dence hero Bernardo O'Higgins and his 120 soldiers, who
sought refuge here after a fight with the Spanish. The finest
products of the estate all carry "120" in their names, as in
"120 Chardonnay" or "120 Sauvignon Blanc". Both are in
fact among the best Chilean wines – just as Domingo
Fernández Concha once hoped they would be.

Book to pack: "The House of the Spirits" by Isabel Allende

Hotel Casa Real	
Viña Santa Rita,	
Camino Padre Hurtado 0695	
Alto Jahuel/Buin	
Chile	
Tel. (56) 28219966 and (56) 28219767	
Website: www.santarita.com	
www.great-escapes-hotels.com	

DIRECTIONS	Situated 25 km/15 miles south of Santiago
RATES	$$
ROOMS	10 double rooms, 6 suites
FOOD	The "Doña Paula" Restaurant serves very good regional and international cuisine. An excellent wine list, including the estate's own range of wines
HISTORY	The property, dating from 1880, converted into a country hotel in 1996
X-FACTOR	Lead the life of a wine-grower – on a choice estates

Sommersitz im Süden

Als Domingo Fernández Concha 1880 das Weingut Santa Rita gründete, ging es ihm nicht nur darum, hier künftig einige der besten Weine Chiles anzubauen – er wollte auch in einem der schönsten Häuser der Nation wohnen. Südlich von Santiago ließ er ein Landhaus de luxe errichten; im pompejanischen Stil, mit prachtvollen Freitreppen, schlanken Säulen und hohen Fenstern. Er residierte unter reich verzierten Holzdecken und Kristalllüstern, blickte in gold-umrahmte Spiegel und auf glänzende Ölgemälde – und besaß sogar einen aus England importierten Billardtisch. All das hochherrschaftliche Flair kann man noch heute genießen, denn seit 1996 ist das Haus das Hotel Casa Real und lädt seine Gäste zu einer Reise in die Vergangenheit ein. Vielleicht noch schöner als anno dazumal ist der Park rund um das Anwesen, den der französische Landschaftsarchitekt Guillermo Renner 1882 anlegte – ein verwunschenes Fleckchen Erde mit jahrhundertealten Zedern, Mandel-, Oliven- und Zitronenbäumen sowie der wahrscheinlich größten Bougainvillea des Kontinents. Zum Hotel gehört außerdem das Doña Paula Restaurant, benannt nach seiner ehemaligen Eigentümerin und eine Hommage an Chiles Unabhängigkeitsheld Bernardo O'Higgins und seine 120 Soldaten, die hier nach einer Schlacht gegen die Spanier Unterschlupf suchten. Die besten Produkte des Hauses tragen alle ein »120« im Namen, zum Beispiel der »120 Chardonnay« oder der »120 Sauvignon Blanc«. Beide gehören übrigens zu den besten Weinen Chiles – ganz im Sinne von Domingo Fernández Concha.

Buchtipp: »Das Geisterhaus« von Isabel Allende

La magie du Sud

Lorsque Domingo Fernandez Concha a fondé le vignoble de Santa Rita en 1880, il ne voulait pas seulement produire ici quelques-uns des meilleurs vins du Chili. Il avait aussi l'intention d'habiter dans l'une des plus belles maisons du pays. Il fit édifier au sud de Santiagoune villa luxueuse de style pompéien, dotée de magnifiques perrons, de colonnes élancées et de hautes fenêtres. Les salons abritaient des plafonds lambrissés richement décorés et des lustres de cristal, des miroirs aux cadres dorés, des tableaux peints à l'huile – et même un billard importé d'Angleterre.
Cette ambiance aristocratique existe toujours. Devenue l'Hotel Casa Real en 1996, la maison invite ses hôtes à voyager dans le temps et à goûter les plaisirs d'une époque disparue. Le parc agencé en 1882 par le paysagiste français Guillermo Renner est peut-être encore plus beau qu'alors. C'est un endroit magique qui abrite des cèdres, des amandiers, des oliviers et des citronniers séculaires ainsi que probablement le plus grand bougainvillée du continent.
Le Doña Paula Restaurant fait partie de l'hôtel. Il doit son nom à son ancienne propriétaire et rend hommage au héros de l'indépendance chilienne Bernardo O'Higgins et à ses 120 soldats qui vinrent se réfugier ici après une bataille contre les troupes espagnoles. Les meilleurs produits de la maison sont tous nommés « 120 » en l'honneur de ces patriotes, par exemple le « 120 Chardonnay » ou le « 120 Sauvignon Blanc ». Ces deux là font partie des meilleurs vins du Chili – Domingo Fernández Concha peut donc dormir tranquille.

Livre à emporter : « La maison aux esprits » d'Isabel Allende

ANREISE	25 Kilometer südlich von Santiago gelegen
PREISE	$$
ZIMMER	10 Doppelzimmer, 6 Suiten
KÜCHE	»Doña Paula« Restaurant mit sehr guter regionaler und internationaler Küche. Ausgezeichnete Weinkarte, hauseigene Vinothek
GESCHICHTE	Anwesen aus dem Jahr 1880, 1996 Umbau zum Landhotel
X-FAKTOR	Wohnen wie ein Winzer – auf einem der besten Weingüter

ACCÈS	Situé à 25 kilomètres au sud de Santiago
PRIX	$$
CHAMBRES	10 chambres doubles, 6 suites
RESTAURATION	Le «Doña Paula » Restaurant propose une savoureuse cuisine régionale et internationale. Remarquable carte des vins, la maison à sa propre cave
HISTOIRE	Domaine datant de 1880, transformé en hôtel de campagne en 1996
LE « PETIT PLUS »	Célébrer la « dive bouteille » dans l'un des meilleurs domaines viticoles

Simply beautiful...
explora en Atacama, Atacama

Simply beautiful

The country below this bleached-out sky is one of the barest and most arid on earth – and one of the most intriguing, too. One feature of the Atacama desert in northern Chile is the Salar de Atacama, a salt lake some 300 square kilometres (74,000 acres) in area, containing vast reserves of lithium and offering a home to rosy-coloured flamingos. There are also mysterious volcanoes affording a suitable challenge to the practised climber, and the Tatio geysers that send great jets of water aloft every morning. Not least among the attractions is the explora en Atacama hotel. Chilean architect Germán de Sol built it at an altitude of 2,400 metres (some 7,500 feet) hard by the oasis village of San Pedro de Atacama. With a main building and three courtyard groupings, it was conceived along the lines of a farmstead. Far from familiar civilisation, it affords every creature comfort, while at the same time reflecting the spartan simplicity of the landscape it is set in. The patios and buildings are linked by plain walkways and steps, large panoramic windows command views of the desert that can be enjoyed even from your bed, and the rooms have been done in regional materials such as black, natural stone. The mild temperatures are perfect for excursions or for the four long, simply-designed pools, massages in the "Casa del Agua" or the "Termas de Puritama", hot springs at an altitude of 3,100 metres (nearly ten thousand feet) some 30 kilometres or 20 miles away. Then at night the hotel has a special treat in store for its guests: on the new "Pueblo de Estrellas" observation platform there are three telescopes to scan the skies above the desert, a smooth expanse of blue-black velvet starred with glittering sequins.

Book to pack: "Clandestine in Chile: The Adventures of Miguel Littin" by Gabriel García Márquez

explora en Atacama
Hotel de Larache
Calle Domingo Atienza S/N,
Ayllú de Larache
Casilla 8
San Pedro de Atacama, Chile
Tel. (56) 22066060
Fax (56) 22284655
E-mail: reservexplora@explora.com
Website: www.explora.com
www.great-escapes-hotels.com

DIRECTIONS	Situated 100 km/63 miles southeast of Calama (regular domestic flights from Santiago de Chile). The one-hour bus transfer is organised
RATES	$$$$
ROOMS	50 double rooms
FOOD	Healthy fare using produce chiefly from the region. At lunch and dinner there are two menus to choose from
HISTORY	Opened 1st September 1998
X-FACTOR	Unlock the secrets of the desert

Schlicht schön

Die Landschaft unter dem weiß schraffierten Himmel ist eine der kargsten und trockensten der Erde – und dennoch eine der faszinierendsten. Die Atacamawüste im Norden Chiles besitzt den rund 300 Quadratkilometer bedeckenden Salzsee Salar de Atacama, der gewaltige Lithiumreserven birgt und Heimat der rosafarbenen Flamingos ist. Sie bietet geheimnisvolle Vulkane, die geübte Bergsteiger sogar bezwingen können, die Tatio-Geysire, die jeden Morgen Wasserfontänen in die Luft fauchen – und nicht zuletzt das Hotel explora en Atacama. Der chilenische Architekt Germán de Sol hat es auf 2.400 Metern Höhe am Rand des Oasendorfs San Pedro de Atacama gebaut und mit einem Haupthaus und drei Höfen wie eine Farm konzipiert. Fern aller gewohnten Zivilisation bietet es jeden Komfort, spiegelt aber zugleich Klarheit und Schlichtheit der umliegenden Landschaft wieder. Einfache Rampen und Treppen verbinden die Patios und die Gebäude, große Fensterfronten geben den Blick auf die Wüste frei (sogar vom Bett aus bietet sich ein zauberhaftes Panorama), und die Zimmer sind mit regionalen Materialien wie schwarzem Naturstein ausgestattet. Die milden Temperaturen genießt man bei Tagesausflügen, an den vier langgezogenen und schnörkellos designten Pools, bei Massagen in der »Casa del Agua« oder in den 30 Kilometer entfernten »Termas de Puritama«, den heißen Quellen auf 3.100 Metern Höhe. Nachts holt das Hotel seinen Gästen dann die Sterne vom Himmel: Von der neuen Plattform »Pueblo de Estrellas« aus kann man mit Hilfe dreier Teleskope einen Blick in den Himmel über der Wüste werfen, der wie schwarzblauer Samt voller glitzernder Pailletten wirkt.

Buchtipp: »Das Abenteuer des Miguel Littín« von Gabriel García Márquez

Beau tout simplement

Le paysage qui s'étend sous le ciel strié de blanc est l'un des plus pauvres et des plus arides de la Terre, et pourtant il est aussi l'un des plus fascinants. C'est sur ce désert d'Atacama, dans le nord du Chili, que se trouve le lac salé, Salar de Atacama, d'une surface de 300 kilomètres carrés, qui est à la fois une énorme réserve de lithium et un refuge pour les flamands roses. Le désert offre aussi ses volcans mystérieux que peuvent escalader des alpinistes expérimentés, ses geysers Tatio qui crachent tous les matins des fontaines d'eau dans les airs – et, last but not least, l'hôtel explora en Atacama. L'architecte chilien Germán de Sol l'a construit à 2.400 mètres d'altitude près du village de San Pedro de Atacama et l'a conçu comme un ranch avec un bâtiment principal et trois annexes. Loin de toute civilisation, il offre beaucoup de confort tout en reflétant la clarté et la sobriété du paysage environnant. Des rampes et des escaliers tout simples relient les patios et les bâtiments, des fenêtres panoramiques donnent sur le désert (on a même une vue splendide de son lit) et les chambres sont décorées avec des matériaux de la région, comme la pierre noire. On profitera des températures agréables pour faire des excursions d'une journée, pour se baigner dans l'un des quatre longs bassins, pour se faire masser dans la «Casa del Agua» ou encore pour se rendre aux «Termas de Puritama», des sources chaudes situées à trente kilomètres de l'hôtel, à 3100 mètres d'altitude. La nuit, l'hôtel fait descendre les étoiles du ciel tout spécialement pour ses clients : sur la nouvelle plate-forme «Pueblo de Estrellas», on peut ainsi à l'aide de trois télescopes regarder le ciel au-dessus du désert qui ressemble alors à du satin bleu foncé parsemé de paillettes étincelantes.

Livre à emporter : «L'aventure de Miguel Littín, clandestin au Chili» de Gabriel García Márquez

ANREISE	100 Kilometer südöstlich von Calama gelegen (dorthin regelmäßige Flugverbindungen ab Santiago de Chile). Einstündiger Bustransfer wird organisiert
PREISE	$$$$
ZIMMER	50 Doppelzimmer
KÜCHE	Gesunde Küche mit vorwiegend regionalen Produkten. Mittags und abends stehen jeweils zwei Menüs zur Auswahl
GESCHICHTE	Am 1. September 1998 eröffnet
X-FAKTOR	Den Geheimnissen der Wüste auf der Spur

ACCÈS	Situé à 100 kilomètres au sud-est de Calama (vols réguliers depuis Santiago de Chile). Le transfert d'une heure en car est organisé
PRIX	$$$$
CHAMBRES	50 chambres doubles
RESTAURATION	Cuisine saine préparée surtout avec des produits de la région. Deux menus au choix le midi et le soir
HISTOIRE	Ouvert depuis le 1er septembre 1998
LE «PETIT PLUS»	Sur les traces des mystères du désert

Built on salt...
Hotel de Sal, Salar de Uyuni

Hotel de Sal, Salar de Uyuni

Built on salt

There are hotels where guests sleep on wooden boards, sacks of straw, or even blocks of ice. And then there's a hotel where you sleep on salt. What's more, you sit on salt chairs and dine at salt tables, and look out through windows cut in walls of salt on a view of never-ending salt flats. Welcome to the Hotel de Sal. At Atulcha, in Bolivia's Salar de Uyuni, Marinko and Rita Ayaviri have created one of South America's most unusual homes from home; there is no electric light, nor any phones or mini-bars, but their hospitality is unbelievable, their sense of the environment is all systems go, and the hotel itself consists almost entirely of the region's abundant natural resource. The Salar de Uyuni is the largest salt desert in the Andes, extending over 12,000 square kilometres (4,600 square miles) and situated at an altitude of about 3,700 metres (about 11,500 feet) between the Eastern and Western Cordilleras. Locals call it the "White Sea", or "Bolivia's Alaska" – up here the air is rarefied, the light is glaring, and the salt crust can be ten metres (more than thirty feet) thick. In the dry season, curious cracks appear in it, and it looks like frozen honeycomb, while in the rainy period from November to March it is sometimes transformed into a treacherous swamp. During those months, visitors unfamiliar with the terrain can easily get lost, and should only venture into the desert in a four-wheel-drive jeep with a navigation system, with a Bolivian guide. Local agencies and tour operators offer several-day excursions into the Salar, including a night in the Hotel de Sal. It's a bumpy ride, and you'll enjoy the candlelit dinner at colourfully decked tables all the more for it. At night your dreams will be filled with the beauties of this unreal landscape, and when you depart you'll realise that paradise can be made of many things, including salt.

Book to pack: "The Feast of the Goat" by Mario Vargas Llosa

Hotel de Sal
Marinko and Rita Ayaviri
c/o Hostal Marith, Avenida Potosí 61
casi esq. Ayacucho
Casilla 23
Uyuni, Bolivia
Tel. and Fax (591) 2 6932174
No E-mail or website
www.great-escapes-hotels.com

DIRECTIONS	Situated 300 km/190 miles northwest of Uyuni. Organised tours of the Salar de Uyuni stop at the hotel
RATES	$
ROOMS	20 double rooms
FOOD	Plain Bolivian fare
HISTORY	The more attractive of two salt hotels in the Salar de Uyuni
X-FACTOR	Completely made of salt

Auf Salz gebaut

Es gibt Hotels, die betten ihre Gäste auf Holzplanken, Strohsäcke oder Eisblöcke – und es gibt ein Hotel, in dem man sogar auf Salz schläft. Mehr noch: Man sitzt auf Salzstühlen an Salztischen und blickt durch in Salzwände gehauene Fenster auf endlose Salzflächen – willkommen im Hotel de Sal. Bei Atulcha, im Salar de Uyuni von Bolivien, haben Marinko und Rita Ayaviri eine der ungewöhnlichsten Unterkünfte Südamerikas geschaffen; ohne elektrisches Licht, ohne Telefon und Minibar, aber mit unglaublicher Gastfreundschaft, Umweltbewusstsein und beinahe ganz aus dem reichhaltigsten Rohstoff der Region. Der Salar de Uyuni ist die größte Salzwüste der Anden, 12.000 Quadratkilometer groß und knapp 3.700 Meter hoch zwischen der Ost- und Westkordillere gelegen. »Weißes Meer« oder »Alaska von Bolivien« nennen die Einheimischen dieses Gebiet auch – hier oben ist die Luft dünn, das Licht gleißend und die Salzkruste bis zu zehn Meter dick. Während der Trockenzeit bekommt sie skurrile Risse und erinnert an gefrorene Bienenwaben, während der Regenfälle zwischen November und März kann sie sich in einen tückischen Sumpf verwandeln – vor allem in diesen Monaten sind Fremde hier verloren und sollten nur im Allradjeep mit Navigationssystem und in Begleitung eines bolivianischen Guides durch die Wüste fahren. Vor Ort bieten diverse Agenturen und Veranstalter mehrtägige Ausflüge durch den Salar an, die für eine Nacht auch im Hotel de Sal Station machen. Nach der holprigen Fahrt genießt man hier ein Abendessen bei Kerzenschein und an mit bunten Stoffen geschmückten Tischen, träumt nachts von den Schönheiten der unwirklichen Landschaft und weiß spätestens bei der Abreise, dass das Paradies auch aus Salz sein kann.

Buchtipp: »Das Fest des Ziegenbocks« von Mario Vargas Llosa

Édifié sur du sel

Certains hôtels font coucher leurs clients sur des planches de bois, des balles de paille ou des blocs de glace – et il y en a un où l'on dort même sur du sel. Mais cela ne s'arrête pas là car on est assis sur des chaises en sel à une table, elle aussi, en sel et à travers les fenêtres percées dans les murs en sel, la vue donne sur des immensités de sel : bienvenue à l'Hotel de Sal. C'est près d'Atulcha, dans le Salar de Uyuni de Bolivie, que Marinko et Rita Ayaviri ont créé l'un des hôtels les plus insolites d'Amérique du Sud ; sans lumière électrique, téléphone ou minibar, mais extrêmement chaleureux, écologique et construit presque exclusivement avec la ressource naturelle la plus abondante de la région. Le Salar de Uyuni est le plus grand désert de sel des Andes. D'une surface de 12.000 kilomètres carrés, il est situé à près de 3.700 mètres d'altitude entre la Cordillère de l'est et celle de l'ouest. Les habitants de cette région le surnomment la « mer blanche » et l'« Alaska de Bolivie » – ici l'air se raréfie, la lumière est éblouissante et la croûte de sel peut atteindre dix mètres d'épaisseur. Pendant la saison sèche, le désert de sel présente des failles d'aspect bizarre qui évoque une ruche gelée tandis que pendant la saison des pluies, entre novembre et mars, il se transforme en un dangereux marécage. C'est surtout durant ces mois que des étrangers se sont perdus. Si l'on désire s'aventurer dans le désert, il est conseillé de le faire dans une jeep équipée d'un système de navigation et en compagnie d'un guide bolivien. Diverses agences proposent des excursions de plusieurs jours à travers le Salar, avec une nuit passée à l'Hotel de Sal. Après une route cahotante, vous serez ravi de savourer un dîner aux chandelles à une table joliment décorée d'étoffes colorées. La nuit vous rêverez des beautés de ce paysage irréel et au moment du départ, vous saurez que le paradis peut être aussi en sel.

Livre à emporter : « La fête au bouc » de Mario Vargas Llosa

ANREISE	300 Kilometer nordwestlich von Uyuni gelegen. Das Hotel wird im Rahmen mehrtägiger, organisierter Touren durch den Salar de Uyuni angefahren
PREISE	$
ZIMMER	20 Doppelzimmer
KÜCHE	Einfache bolivianische Gerichte
GESCHICHTE	Eines von zwei Salzhotels im Salar de Uyuni – das schönere!
X-FAKTOR	Alles ist Salz

ACCÈS	Situé à 300 kilomètres au nord-ouest d'Uyuni. Les excursions de plusieurs jours à travers le Salar prévoient un arrêt à l'hôtel
PRIX	$
CHAMBRES	20 chambres doubles
RESTAURATION	Plats boliviens simples
HISTOIRE	L'un des deux hôtels de sel dans le Salar de Uyuni – celui-ci est le plus beau !
LE « PETIT PLUS »	Tout est en sel

In the footsteps of history...
Hotel Monasterio, Cuzco

Hotel Monasterio, Cuzco

In the footsteps of history

In the 15th century, when the Incas put up the first buildings in Cuzco, they were not founding anything so humble
as a mere capital. Cuzco was their holy site, and the very
centre of their universe. The city retained its pride in the
years of Spanish colonial rule, and now, with a place on the
UNESCO World Heritage schedule, it is one of South America's most important and diverse cities. If you want to savour
history to the full here, at an altitude of 3,300 metres (over
10,000 feet) and with the Andes affording a stupendous
backdrop, the Hotel Monasterio is the place to stay. Built in
1592 as a monastery, it is perhaps the loveliest habitable
museum in all Peru – the venerable walls within which you
dwell are so thick, it's as if you needed protecting from the
outside world. When you walk beneath the rounded arches
of the cloisters, it can almost come as a disappointment not
to encounter a monk around the next corner. The ground
plan of the former monastic cells, shared halls and chapel
has remained largely unaltered – but the spartan appointments are a thing of the past. No two rooms in the Hotel
Monasterio are alike. In one you sit on a majestic deep-plush
armchair; in another hangs a splendid gilt-framed painting.
There are costly antiques, gleaming mirrors and crystal
chandeliers. From cable television to mini-bars, the rooms
have every modern comfort, and now even offer an enriched
oxygen supply for those who may suffer from altitude sick-
ness. After a night in the Monasterio's "oxygen tent" you'll
have no problems enjoying the magic of Cuzco or taking the
trip to Machu Picchu – the "lost city of the Incas" is just a
three-and-a-half-hour train ride away.

Book to pack: "Death in the Andes" by Mario Vargas Llosa

Hotel Monasterio	
Calle Palacios 136, Plazoleta Nazarenas	
Cuzco	
Peru	
Tel. (51) 84604000	
Fax (51) 84604001	
E-mail: info@peruorientexpress.com.pe	
Website: www.monasterio.orient-express.com	
www.great-escapes-hotels.com	

DIRECTIONS	Located in the heart of Cuzco, 10 min. from the airport
RATES	$$$$
ROOMS	109 double rooms, 12 Junior Suites, 1 Deluxe Suite, 3 Presidential Suites, 2 Royal Suites
FOOD	3 restaurants serving Peruvian and international cuisine. The most attractive is "El Tupay" with its festive Inca Dinner
HISTORY	Built in 1592 as a monastery, a hotel since 1995
X-FACTOR	History at close quarters

Wandeln auf historischen Wegen

Als die Inka im 15. Jahrhundert die ersten Häuser von Cuzco errichteten, gründeten sie weit mehr als eine einfache Hauptstadt – Cuzco war ihr Heiligtum und das Zentrum ihrer Welt. Die Stadt behielt ihren Stolz auch während der spanischen Kolonialherrschaft und gehört als Unesco-Weltkulturerbe heute zu den wichtigsten und vielfältigsten Stätten Südamerikas. Wer hier, auf 3.300 Metern Höhe und vor einer beeindruckenden Andenkulisse, in die Historie eintauchen möchte, zieht am besten ins Hotel Monasterio. Aus dem 1592 erbauten Kloster ist das vielleicht schönste bewohnbare Museum in Peru geworden – man lebt hinter altehrwürdigen Mauern, die so dick sind, als müssten sie ihre Gäste vor der Außenwelt schützen, wandelt durch von Rundbögen gesäumte Kreuzgänge und ist beinahe enttäuscht, wenn einem hinter der nächsten Ecke kein Mönch entgegenkommt. Der Grundriss der einstigen Zellen, der Versammlungsräume und der Kapelle wurde kaum verändert – die spartanische Ausstattung aber ist Vergangenheit. Im Hotel Monasterio gleicht kein Raum dem anderen; hier thront ein plüschiger Sessel, dort prangt ein goldumrahmtes Gemälde; es gibt wertvolle Antiquitäten, blitzblank geputzte Spiegel und Kristallleuchter. Vom Kabelfernsehen bis zur Minibar sind die Zimmer mit allem modernen Komfort ausgestattet und können seit neuestem sogar mit Sauerstoff angereichert werden, um der unangenehmen Höhenkrankheit vorzubeugen. Nach einer Nacht unter der »Sauerstoffdusche« kann man sich ganz ohne Beschwerden von der Magie Cuzcos verzaubern lassen oder einen Ausflug nach Machu Picchu unternehmen – die »verlorene Stadt der Inka« liegt nur eine dreieinhalbstündige Zugfahrt entfernt.

Buchtipp: »Tod in den Anden« von Mario Vargas Llosa

Suivre les chemins de l'histoire

Lorsque les Incas bâtirent au 15e siècle les premières maisons de Cuzco, ils ne fondèrent pas seulement une capitale – Cuzco était pour eux un lieu sacré et le centre de leur univers. La ville qui garda toute sa fierté même sous la domination des Espagnols, est classée aujourd'hui au patrimoine mondial de l'Unesco. Elle fait partie des sites les plus importants et les plus pittoresques d'Amérique du Sud. Celui qui désire remonter dans le temps, résidera à l'hôtel Monasterio, situé à 3.300 mètres d'altitude dans le décor imposant de la cordillère des Andes. Cet ancien monastère datant de 1592 est peut-être le plus beau musée habitable du Pérou. Protégé du monde extérieur par d'épaisses murailles, l'hôte se promène à travers les arcades du cloître et il est presque déçu de ne rencontrer aucun moine au détour de son chemin. Si le plan des cellules, des salles communes et de la chapelle n'a pratiquement pas subi de modifications, l'équipement spartiate fait lui bien partie du passé. À l'hôtel Monasterio, aucune pièce ne ressemble à une autre. Ici trône un fauteuil en peluche, là resplendit le cadre doré d'un tableau. Chaque pièce recèle des antiquités précieuses. Les chambres sont équipées du confort moderne, qui va du câble au minibar, et depuis peu, elles sont même alimentées en oxygène afin d'éviter les effets indésirables de l'altitude. Après une nuit sous la « douche à oxygène » on pourra alors succomber sans problèmes à la magie de Cuzco ou entreprendre une excursion jusqu'à Machu Picchu – la « ville perdue des Incas » n'est en effet qu'à trois-quarts d'heure de train.

Livre à emporter : « Lituma dans les Andes »
de Mario Vargas Llosa

ANREISE	Im Zentrum von Cuzco gelegen, 10 Fahrminuten vom Flughafen entfernt
PREISE	$$$$
ZIMMER	109 Doppelzimmer, 12 Junior Suiten, 1 Deluxe Suite, 3 Präsidenten-Suiten, 2 Royal Suiten
KÜCHE	3 Restaurants mit peruanischer und internationaler Küche. Am schönsten ist »El Tupay« mit seinem festlichen Inka-Dinner
GESCHICHTE	1592 als Kloster erbaut, seit 1995 ein Hotel
X-FAKTOR	Wo man Historie hautnah erlebt

ACCÈS	Situé dans le centre de Cuzco, 10 min. de l'aéroport
PRIX	$$$$
CHAMBRES	109 chambres doubles, 12 suites junior, 1 suite de luxe, 3 suites présidentielles, 2 suites royales
RESTAURATION	3 restaurants proposant une cuisine péruvienne et internationale. Le plus beau est « El Tupay » avec son dîner inca
HISTOIRE	Monastère construit en 1592, hôtel depuis 1995
LE « PETIT PLUS »	Un lieu où l'on peut revivre le passé

An unfamiliar way of life...
Kapawi Ecolodge & Reserve, Pastaza

An unfamiliar way of life

It is hidden away in the rain forest, the only "road" leading to it is a waterway, and the nearest sizeable town is a ten-day foot-slog away: the Kapawi Ecolodge is about as far from everything as you could imagine. A visit here in the jungles of Ecuador affords natural wonders seen not even in *National Geographic* photos, and a glimpse of the world of the Achuar. For the Lodge was built by a private venture, Canodros, together with the indigenous people, and in the year 2011 it will belong to them outright. It is a unique ecological and community project, intended to assure the Achuar people a new living area without their being required to forfeit their traditional homes. The 20 cottages, tucked away between the greenery and the Kapawi Lagoon, are built up on stilts in the customary way, thatched with straw, and powered with solar energy. It's a surprisingly comfortable place to stay (even if occasionally shared with animal fellow "guests" from the jungle), but the cosiness is always accompanied by a sense of genuine adventure. A typical day may begin with birdwatching at six on the bank of the Capahuari River, trekking, and a picnic in the tropical scenery in the afternoon, and at night caymans. Depending on how fit visitors are, the Lodge offers easy, middling, or tough excursions – always including a visit to the Achuar people. Their villages, and their company, afford an insight into an unfamiliar way of life, in an unfamiliar world – and afterwards the philosophy of Kapawi makes even better sense.

Book to pack: "The Jívaro: People of the Sacred Waterfalls" by Michael Harner

Kapawi Ecolodge & Reserve	
c/o Edificio Reina Victoria, Piso 1, Oficina 2	
Mariscal Foch E7-38 y Reina Victoria	
Quito	
Ecuador	
Tel. (59) 326009333	
Fax (59) 326009334	
E-mail: info@kapawi.com	
Website: www.kapawi.com	
www.great-escapes-hotels.com	

DIRECTIONS	Situated 300 km/188 miles southeast of Quito. The transfer by plane and canoe is organised
RATES	$$
ROOMS	20 double rooms in cottages with bath and veranda
FOOD	Ecuadorian and international cooking, using regional produce. Suitable for vegetarians
HISTORY	Built in 1993 jointly with the Achuar. In 2011 the indigenous people will own the Lodge outright
X-FACTOR	Ecotourism of first-class standard

Spiegelbild einer fremden Kultur

Sie versteckt sich mitten im Regenwald, die einzige »Straße«, die zu ihr führt, ist ein Wasserweg, und zur nächsten
größeren Stadt sind es zehn Tagesmärsche: Die Kapawi Ecolodge liegt am Ende unseres räumlichen Vorstellungsvermö-
gens. Wer hierher reist, erlebt im Dschungel Ecuadors
Naturschauspiele, wie er sie nicht einmal von den Fotos im
»National Geographic« her kannte, und bekommt eine
Ahnung von der Welt der Achuar. Denn die Lodge wurde
vom Privatunternehmen Canodros zusammen mit den Ein-
geborenen erbaut und wird ihnen im Jahr 2011 ganz gehören – als einzigartiges Öko- und Communityprojekt, das den
Achuar neuen Lebensraum sichern soll, ohne dass sie ihren
traditionellen aufgeben müssen. Die 20 Hütten zwischen
dichtem Grün und der Kapawi Lagune sind nach überliefer-
ter Art auf Stelzen gebaut, damit der Boden nicht mehr als
nötig belastet wird, mit Stroh gedeckt und mit Solarenergie
versorgt. Man wohnt überraschend komfortabel (wenn auch
von Zeit zu Zeit in Gesellschaft tierischer Dschungel»gäste«),
hat aber bei aller Annehmlichkeit immer das Gefühl, ein
echtes Abenteuer zu bestehen. Zum Beispiel, wenn es
morgens um sechs Uhr zum Birdwatching am Ufer des
Capahuari-Flusses geht, mittags eine Trekkingtour mit
Picknick in tropischer Kulisse auf dem Programm steht
oder nachts die Kaimane auftauchen. Je nach Kondition der
Gäste bietet die Lodge leichte, mittlere oder anspruchsvolle
Exkursionen an – inbegriffen ist immer auch ein Besuch bei
den Achuar. In ihren Dörfern und in ihrer Gesellschaft lässt
man sich von einer fremden Lebensart in einer fremden
Welt faszinieren – und versteht die Philosophie von Kapawi
anschließend noch ein bisschen besser.
Buchtipp: »Jivaro« von Jörgen Bitsch

Retour aux sources

Difficile de se représenter l'emplacement du Kapawi Lodge,
dissimulé au cœur de la forêt, et auquel on n'accède que par
voie d'eau, la grande ville la plus proche se trouvant à dix
jours de marche. Celui qui séjourne ici dans la jungle écua-
dorienne peut contempler des spectacles naturels que même
« National Geographic » n'a pas photographiés, et découvrir
l'univers des Achuar. En effet, le Lodge a été construit par
l'entrepreneur Canodros en collaboration avec les autochtones et il leur appartiendra complètement en 2011. Ce projet communautaire et écologique unique en son genre doit
assurer aux Achuar un nouvel espace vital sans qu'ils doivent renoncer à leur mode de vie traditionnel.
Les vingt huttes édifiées entre la végétation luxuriante et la
lagune de Kapawi sont construites sur pilotis comme le
veulent les traditions Achuar, cette méthode évitant que le
sol soit trop chargé. Elles sont couvertes de paille et ravi-
taillées en énergie solaire. On y vit de manière étonnam-
ment confortable (quoique les animaux de la jungle n'hési-
tent pas à s'inviter sans façons) sans toutefois perdre la
sensation de vivre une aventure authentique et de devoir
faire ses preuves. C'est le cas le matin à six heures quand
on part observer les oiseaux sur les rives de la Capahuari, le
midi pendant la randonnée avec pique-nique dans un décor
tropical et la nuit quand les caïmans se réveillent.
Le Lodge offre des excursions adaptées à la forme physique
de chacun – faciles, moyennes et difficiles – mais elles com-
portent toujours une visite chez les Achuar. Dans leur village
et en leur compagnie on est fasciné par un mode de vie qui
nous est étranger dans un monde qui nous est tout aussi
peu familier. Ensuite on comprend mieux encore la philosophie de Kapawi.
Livre à emporter : « Les Jivaros » de Michael J. Harner

ANREISE	300 Kilometer südöstlich von Quito gelegen. Der Transfer per Flugzeug und Kanu wird organisiert	
PREISE	$$	
ZIMMER	20 Doppelzimmer in Hütten; mit Bad und Veranda	
KÜCHE	Ecuadorianische und internationale Küche, mit Produkten aus der Region. Auch für Vegetarier	
GESCHICHTE	1993 gemeinsam mit den Achuar erbaut. 2011 werden die Eingeborenen die Lodge ganz besitzen	
X-FAKTOR	Ökotourismus erster Klasse	

ACCÈS	Situé à 300 kilomètres au sud-est de Quito. Le trans-fert en avion et en canot est organisé
PRIX	$$
CHAMBRES	20 chambres doubles dans des huttes ; avec salle de bains et véranda
RESTAURATION	Cuisine écuadorienne et internationale avec des pro-duits de la région. Menus végétariens
HISTOIRE	Construit avec les Achuar en 1993. En 2011, le Lodge entrera en possession des autochtones
LE « PETIT PLUS »	Tourisme vert de première classe

Pictures of paradise...
Hotel San Pedro de Majagua, Islas del Rosario

Pictures of paradise

In 1955, off the coast of Columbia, French artist Pierre Daguet found his very own personal paradise: the Isla Grande, where the trees stood so close that the canopy of their crowns was a heaven of green. where the beaches were of white sand, and where the crystal-clear sea all around was rifted with brightly-coloured coral reefs. Diving beneath the waves, Daguet seemingly found not only exotic fish but also mysterious "Ondinas" – shimmering water nymphs that he immortalised in his paintings. Today, where once there were easels in his erstwhile studio, there are now surfboards and sailboats – for the humble cabin now serves as a boat-house for the Hotel San Pedro de Majagua. The accommodation is in 17 pretty *cabanas*, the all-natural roofs of which look as if over-long fringes were curtaining their faces. On their terraces you can relax in striped hammocks, deep wooden armchairs, or bright red sofas. Inside, the cottages are appointed with purist simplicity, with clear lines, select dark pieces of furniture, and fabrics in light colours – but there's fun too, with amusing notes struck by a stone tortoise on the floor, or an orange starfish on the wall. You could easily pass the days here walking the island, gazing out upon the glittering sea, and dreaming of Daguet's nymphs... The artist's memory is preserved not only in his lively paintings but also in testimony to his capacity for drink: just a few metres off the beach, all the wine bottles he emptied in the course of well-nigh 30 years with friends and in high carousals are submerged under the waves – they have now become a coral reef in their own right, known to the locals as the "Bajo de las Botellas de Daguet".

Book to pack: "The Story of a Shipwrecked Sailor"
by Gabriel García Márquez

Hotel San Pedro de Majagua	
Isla Grande	
Islas del Rosario	
Colombia	
Tel. (57) 56646070 and (57) 16228246	
Website: www.hotelmajagua.com	
www.great-escapes-hotels.com	

DIRECTIONS	Situated on Isla Grande (Islas del Rosario National Park), 45 minutes by boat southwest of Cartagena de Indias
RATES	$
ROOMS	4 Cabanas Suites, 10 Cabanas Playa, 3 Cabanas Laguna
FOOD	Restaurant serving first-class seafood
HISTORY	Centred on the former studio of artist Pierre Daguet
X-FACTOR	For latter-day Crusoes and enthusiastic divers

Bilder vom Paradies

Vor der Küste Kolumbiens fand der französische Maler Pierre Daguet 1955 sein ganz persönliches Paradies: die Isla Grande, auf der die Bäume so dicht standen, dass ihre Kronen einen grünen Himmel bildeten, die weiße Sandstrände besaß und von einem kristallklaren Meer umgeben war, das bunte Korallenriffe barg. Bei seinen Tauchausflügen in die Unterwasserwelt scheint Daguet neben exotischen Fischen auch geheimnisvolle »Ondinas« getroffen zu haben – die schillernden Nixen jedenfalls verewigte er zurück an Land auf farbenprächtigen Bildern. Heute stehen in seinem ehemaligen Atelier statt der Staffeleien jede Menge Surfbretter und Segelboote – denn die kleine Hütte ist das Bootshaus des Hotels San Pedro de Majagua geworden. Zu ihm gehören 17 hübsche Cabanas, die mit ihren naturgedeckten Dächern so aussehen, als hingen ihnen überlange Ponyfransen ins Gesicht, und auf deren Terrassen man in gestreiften Hängematten, tiefen Holzsesseln oder auf knallroten Sofas entspannt. Innen sind die Häuschen mit klaren Linien, ausgesuchten dunklen Möbeln und hellen Stoffen recht puristisch – doch Accessoires wie eine steinerne Schildkröte auf dem Boden oder ein orangefarbener Seestern an der Wand setzen amüsante Akzente. Die Tage ließen sich ohne weiteres damit verbringen, über die Insel zu spazieren, auf die glitzernde See zu schauen und von Daguets Nixen zu träumen ... Doch man sollte auch an anderer Stelle des Künstlers gedenken, der nicht nur bunt zeichnen, sondern auch viel trinken konnte: Wenige Meter vom Strand entfernt wurden alle Weinflaschen im Meer versenkt, die er in fast 30 Jahren gemeinsam mit Freunden und bei rauschenden Festen geleert hatte – inzwischen bilden sie eine Korallenbank, die bei den Einheimischen auch unter dem Namen »Bajo de las Botellas de Daguet« bekannt ist.

Buchtipp: »Bericht eines Schiffbrüchigen« von Garbiel García Márquez

Images du Paradis

C'est au large de la côte colombienne que le peintre français Pierre Daguet a trouvé son paradis en 1955 : l'Isla Grande avec ses arbres si nombreux que leurs couronnes formaient une voûte de verdure, ses plages de sable blanc, ses eaux cristallines et ses bancs de coraux multicolores. Au cours d'une de ses plongées sous-marines, Daguet semble avoir rencontré des poissons exotiques, mais aussi de mystérieuses ondines qu'il immortalisa sur ses toiles aux couleurs magnifiques. Aujourd'hui, son ancien atelier ne contient plus de tableaux, mais une foule de planches à voile et de bateaux car la petite cabane est devenue l'annexe nautique de l'hôtel San Pedro de Majagua. Celui-ci comprend 17 jolies « cabanas » qui, avec leurs toits végétaux, semblent avoir une frange qui leur tombe sur le visage. Sur leurs terrasses, les hamacs rayés, les profonds fauteuils en bois et les canapés rouge vif invitent à la détente. À l'intérieur, les maisonnettes affichent un air puriste avec leurs meubles sombres aux lignes sobres et leurs étoffes claires, mais les accessoires comme une tortue de pierre posée sur le sol ou une étoile orange accrochée au mur ajoutent une note amusante. On pourrait tout aussi bien passer ses journées à se promener sur l'île, à regarder les flots scintillants et à rêver des naïades de Daguet... Mais on peut également rendre un autre hommage à la mémoire du peintre qui n'aimait pas seulement les couleurs vives, mais aussi la dive bouteille, en allant voir ce que les habitants de l'île ont appelé le « Bajo de las Botellas de Daguet » : à quelques mètres de la plage, on a en effet immergé toutes les bouteilles de vin que le peintre et ses amis ont bues en 30 ans, au cours de leurs mémorables fêtes. Toutes ces bouteilles forment maintenant une véritable barrière de corail.

Livre à emporter : « Chronique d'une mort annoncée »
de Gabriel García Márquez

ANREISE	Auf Isla Grande (Nationalpark Islas del Rosario) gelegen, 45 Bootsminuten südwestlich von Cartagena de Indias
PREISE	$
ZIMMER	4 Cabanas Suites, 10 Cabanas Playa, 3 Cabanas Laguna
KÜCHE	Restaurant mit erstklassigem Seafood
GESCHICHTE	Rings um das ehemalige Atelier von Pierre Daguet gebaut
X-FAKTOR	Für Robinsons Nachfahren und begeisterte Taucher

ACCÈS	Situé sur Isla Grande (parc national Islas del Rosario), à 45 minutes en bateau au sud-ouest de Cartagena de Indias
PRIX	$
CHAMBRES	4 Cabanas Suites, 10 Cabanas Playa, 3 Cabanas Laguna
RESTAURATION	Restaurant proposant des fruits de mer de premier choix
HISTOIRE	Construit autour de l'ancien atelier de Pierre Daguet
LE « PETIT PLUS »	Pour les descendants de Robinson Crusoë et les passionnés de plongée

MAJAGUA
-CAUCHO-

› **activesouthamerica.com**
The perfect page for adventurers in search of an active, adrenaline-packed vacation in Peru, Patagonia and Ecuador. You can book a trekking tour on the "Inca Trail" to Machu Picchu, a night on an Indio island in Lake Titicaca, or a trip into the jungle complete with piranha fish.

› **boliviaweb.com**
The A to Z of Bolivia. All you need to know about entering and leaving the country, the weather and the best times to travel, hotels and restaurants, and the major sights. For those who enjoy cooking themselves, there are even Bolivian recipes.

› **brol.com**
Economical offers for vacations in Brazil (particularly for travellers from North America) and numerous extras such as the Rio carnival or birdwatching on Fernando de Noronha.

› **chile.com**
The whole country at a glance – this website has up-to-the-minute information on the politics, economy, and culture of Chile, in both Spanish and English. For tourists there are contact details of hotels, travel operators and car hire companies. There is also a photo gallery.

› **ecuadorexplorer.com**
An all-round, up-to-date page. Alongside basics such as entering the country and finding accommodation, it has information on more unusual things to do, from riding or diving holidays to Spanish courses in Ecuador. Includes a substantial section on the Galapagos Islands.

› **gochile.cl**
Paints a brilliant picture of the diversity of vacation options in Chile: from walking in the Torres des Paine National Park to cruises to skiing holidays, the website presents a vast array of temptations and lists offers to suit the budget traveller.

› **gosouthamerica.about.com**
The perfect way to get in the South American mood on a rainy day at home. There are articles about the most beautiful destinations around the continent together with information on the history, culture, and cuisine. The site also has up-to-date news plus extras such as tips for honeymooners.

› **latindiscover.com**
Specialist site for travel in Central and South America. From a tango weekend in Buenos Aires to trekking in the Perito Moreno glacier to rafting near Iguazu, it is all just waiting to be booked.

› **literatura.org**
A superb site for aficionados of Argentine literature. There are portraits of all the

› **activesouthamerica.com**
Die richtige Seite für Aktivurlauber, die in Peru und Ecuador den Adrenalinkick suchen. Sie können zum Beispiel ein Trekking auf dem »Inca Trail« nach Machu Picchu buchen, eine Nacht auf einer Indianer-Insel im Titicaca-See oder einen Dschungelausflug inklusive Piranha-Fischen.

› **boliviaweb.com**
Ein Land von A bis Z: Diese Website informiert über An- und Einreisebestimmungen, Wetter und Reisezeiten, Hotels und Restaurants sowie die wichtigsten Sehenswürdigkeiten. Extra für Hobbyköche: Bolivianische Rezepte.

› **brol.com**
Preiswerte Angebote für Ferien in Brasilien (vor allem für Reisende aus Nordamerika) und zahlreiche Extras wie Karneval in Rio und Birdwatching auf Fernando de Noronha.

› **chile.com**
Ein Land im Überblick – diese Website bietet aktuelle Informationen aus Politik, Wirtschaft sowie Kultur; und das auf Spanisch und Englisch. Für Touristen gibt es neben Adressen von Hotels, Reiseveranstaltern und Autovermietern auch eine Fotogalerie.

› **ecuadorexplorer.com**
Umfassend und aktuell: Neben Basics wie Anreise und Unterkunft findet man auf dieser Seite auch ungewöhnlichere Angebote wie Reiterferien, Tauchurlaub und Spanischkurse in Ecuador. Mit großem Kapitel über die Galapagos-Inseln.

› **gochile.cl**
So vielfältig können Ferien in Chile sein: Vom Wandern im Nationalpark Torres des Paine über Kreuzfahrten bis hin zum Ski-urlaub stellt die Website zahlreiche Möglichkeiten vor und liefert die passenden Offerten für Budget-Traveller dazu.

› **gosouthamerica.about.com**
Perfekt zum Einlesen an einem verregneten Nachmittag. Hier sind Artikel über die schönsten Ziele in Südamerika gesammelt und werden mit Informationen über Geschichte, Kultur und Küche ergänzt. Außerdem im Angebot: Aktuelle News und Extras wie Tipps für die Flitterwochen.

› **latindiscover.com**
Spezialisiert auf Reisen in Mittel- und Südamerika. Vom Tango-Wochenende in Buenos Aires über das Mini-Trekking im Gletschergebiet um den Perito Moreno bis hin zum Rafting in der Nähe von Iguazu ist alles buchbar.

› **literatura.org**
Eine sehr gute Empfehlung für Fans argentinischer Literatur. Hier werden alle wichtigen zeitgenössischen Autoren porträtiert

› **activesouthamerica.com**
Le site idéal pour les vacanciers actifs qui recherchent une décharge d'adrénaline au Pérou et en Équateur. Possibilités par exemple de réserver un trekking sur le « chemin des Incas » jusqu'à Machu Picchu, de passer une nuit sur une île du lac Titicaca ou de faire une excursion dans la jungle, pêche aux piranhas comprise.

› **boliviaweb.com**
Le pays de A à Z: Ce site vous propose toutes sortes d'informations conditions pour l'entrée et le séjour en Bolivie, la météo, les meilleurs moments de l'année pour voyager, les hôtels, les restaurants et les curiosités touristiques les plus importantes. Tout spécialement pour ceux qui aiment cuisiner des recettes boliviennes.

› **brol.com**
Offres de vacances bon marché au Brésil (surtout pour les voyageurs venant d'Amérique du Nord) et nombreux suppléments comme le carnaval de Rio et l'observation des oiseaux à Fernando de Noronha.

› **chile.com**
Vision d'ensemble du pays. Ce site vous offre des informations actuelles sur la politique, l'économie et la culture en espagnol et en anglais. Pour les touristes il propose des adresses d'hôtels, d'agences de voyages, de location de voitures et une galerie de photos.

› **ecuadorexplorer.com**
Complet et actuel. Outre les informations élémentaires sur le voyage et le logement, vous trouverez sur ce site des idées de vacances originales, comme des séjours équestres, des séjours de plongée et des séjours linguistiques en Équateur. Consacre un important chapitre aux îles de Galapagos.

› **gochile.cl**
De la variété pour vos vacances au Chili : nombreuses possibilités de séjours excitants, allant des excursions dans le parc national Torres des Paine aux séjours de ski, en passant par les croisières. Pour toutes les bourses.

› **gosouthamerica.about.com**
Parfait pour se faire une idée de l'Amérique du Sud un après-midi de pluie. Présentation des plus belles destinations et renseignements sur l'histoire, la culture et la gastronomie. Propose également des suppléments comme l'organisation de votre voyage de noces par exemple.

› **latindiscover.com**
Spécialiste des voyages en Amérique centrale et en Amérique du Sud. Du weekend tango à Buenos Aires au rafting près d'Iguazú, en passant par un mini trekking dans les glaciers de Perito Morino, tout est possible.

TASCHEN Web Picks: Go surfing in South America – a whole fascinating continent is only a click or two away! The Web tips on these pages will take you to the great cities of Argentina and Brazil, to the peaks

major contemporary authors and thumbnail introductions to their latest publications. You do need to read Spanish, though, as the site has no English translation.

> lonelyplanet.com
For 30 years, Lonely Planet has produced some of the best travel guides the world has to offer. Naturally the programme includes South America, in print and online. The sightseeing, hotel, and book tips are continually updated, as are – where appropriate – critical comments on the political and economic aspects of the continent.

> peru.info
Welcome to the realm of the Incas! This page provides a wealth of information on the history of Peru, its finest monuments, sites, and natural splendours, and destinations for those in search of an active vacation. An outstanding plus is that the information is in six languages.

> planeta.com
A field guide to help you through the jungle of eco-tourism. Tour operators as well as regional authorities showcase their environmentally friendly offers here. For South America there are travel operators from Brazil and Ecuador, for instance, with specialist programmes for those wanting to visit the Amazon basin.

> rainforestweb.org
Comprehensive information relating to rain forests worldwide. The Amazon naturally figures prominently – alongside travel tips, there are sections on deforestation and environmental protection. Good links.

> saexplorers.org
The Association of South American Explorers (SAE) provides not only extensive travel information but also a host of things well worth knowing about the nature, economy, and culture of the continent. If you like what you see, you can subscribe to the SAE magazine or become a member of the club yourself.

> spanishunlimited.com
Travelling in South America is twice as enjoyable if you know the language. This page affords a free online opportunity to learn Spanish.

> taschen.com
Like to know more about TASCHEN books? This site lays out the publisher's full portfolio – along with travel titles there are books on design, architecture, art, fashion, popular culture, cinema, and photography waiting to be discovered.

und neue Titel vorgestellt. Allerdings muss man Spanisch können – die Seite kommt ohne englische Übersetzung aus.

> lonelyplanet.com
Seit 30 Jahren einer der besten Reiseführer der Welt; gedruckt und online widmet er sich natürlich auch Südamerika. Und das mit ständig aktualisierten Sightseeing-, Hotel und Literaturtipps sowie – sofern sie eben angebracht sind – kritischen Anmerkungen zu Politik und Wirtschaft.

> peru.info
Willkommen im Reich der Inka! Mit Hilfe dieser Seite erfährt man viel über die Geschichte Perus, die schönsten Denkmäler und Landschaften sowie Ziele für Aktivurlauber. Serviceplus: Die Informationen werden in sechs Sprachen angeboten.

> planeta.com
Ein Wegweiser durch den Dschungel des Ökotourismus. Hier können Reiseveranstalter und Regionen ihre umweltfreundlichen Angebote vorstellen. Für Südamerika sind zum Beispiel Touroperator aus Brasilien und Ecuador mit dabei, die sich auf das Amazonasgebiet spezialisiert haben.

> rainforestweb.org
Umfassende Informationen über die Regenwälder in aller Welt. Auch der Amazonas spielt eine große Rolle – neben Reisetipps werden die Kapitel »Rodung« und »Umweltschutz« aufgenommen. Gute weiterführende Links.

> saexplorers.org
Der Verein South American Explorers (SAE) bietet nicht nur umfangreiche Reiseinformationen, sondern auch Wissenswertes über Natur, Wirtschaft und Kultur des Kontinents. Wer auf den Geschmack gekommen ist, kann das SAE-Magazin abonnieren oder selbst Mitglied im Club werden.

> spanishunlimited.com
Eine Reise durch Südamerika macht doppelt so viel Spaß, wenn man die Sprache beherrscht. Mit Hilfe dieser Seite kann man online und kostenfrei Spanisch lernen.

> taschen.com
Lust auf mehr TASCHEN-Bücher? Hier wird das komplette Portfolio des Verlags präsentiert – neben Titeln zum Thema Reise warten Bücher über Design, Architektur, Kunst, Mode, Popkultur, Film und Fotografie auf Entdecker.

> literatura.org
À recommander pour les fans de la littérature argentine. Portraits d'auteurs contemporains et présentation de nouveaux titres. Ce site est uniquement en espagnol.

> lonelyplanet.com
L'un des meilleurs guides de voyage du monde entier depuis 30 ans qui se consacre également sur le web à l'Amérique du Sud. Actualise en permanence ses renseignements sur les visites guidées, les hôtels et la littérature du pays. Propose quand il y a lieu, des remarques critiques sur la politique et l'économie.

> peru.info
Bienvenue au royaume des Incas. Ce site vous apprendra une foule de choses sur l'histoire du Pérou, les plus beaux monuments, les paysages et les destinations pour des vacances actives. Toutes ces informations sont proposées en six langues.

> planeta.com
Vous aidera à vous y retrouver dans la jungle du tourisme écologique. Les agences de voyage et les régions peuvent présenter leurs offres sur ce site. Pour l'Amérique du Sud, on trouvera par exemple des tour opérateurs du Brésil et de l'Équateur spécialisés dans la région amazonienne.

> rainforestweb.org
Informations complètes sur les forêts tropicales du monde entier. L'Amazone joue aussi un grand rôle. Chapitres sur les idées de voyage, mais aussi consacrés au déboisement et à la protection de l'environnement. Indique des sites web intéressants.

> saexplorers.org
L'association South American Explorers (SAE) offre non seulement des informations sur les voyages mais aussi des renseignements sur la nature, l'économie et la culture du continent. Si vous désirez en savoir plus, vous pouvez vous abonner au magazine ou devenir membre du club.

> spanishunlimited.com
Un voyage à travers l'Amérique du Sud est encore plus agréable quand on maîtrise la langue. Sur ce site vous pourrez apprendre gratuitement l'espagnol.

> taschen.com
Vous voulez connaître encore mieux les livres TASCHEN Voici le programme complet de la maison d'édition avec ses ouvrages sur le thème des voyages, mais aussi sur le design, l'architecture, l'art, la mode, la culture pop, le cinéma et la photographie.

of Patagonia, and the jungle of Ecuador. If the love of South America is in your bones too, you can go on-line for information on the arts and cultures of the continent or even to learn Spanish or Portuguese.

› **travel-library.com/south_america/**
Features extensive links to online travel guides, photo galleries, and maps. The South American impressions of amateur travel writers are also featured here.

› **visit-uruguay.com**
If you're looking for a hotel in one of Uruguay's vacation centres, this is the site for you. As well as reservation information it provides a virtual tour of Montevideo, bus timetables, and contact details of car hire companies.

› **wnsouthamerica.com**
Almost as good as having your own news ticker from a news galleries. This site provides news from every sector, and from every South American country. It includes links to photo galleries, radio stations, and travel operators from Argentina to Uruguay.

› **travel-library.com/south_america/**
Mit vielen Links zu Online-Reiseführern, Fotogalerien und Landkarten. Hobbyschriftsteller haben hier außerdem ihre Erfahrungen aus Südamerika festgehalten.

› **visit-uruguay.com**
Wer in Uruguays Ferienzentren ein Hotel sucht, ist hier richtig. Außer Buchungsinformationen gibt es eine virtuelle Tour durch Montevideo, Busfahrpläne und Adressen von Autovermietern.

› **wnsouthamerica.com**
Fast so gut wie der Newsticker einer Nachrichtenagentur. Hier kann man News aus allen Bereichen und aus allen Ländern abrufen. Inklusive Links zu Fotogalerien, Radiosendern und Reiseveranstaltern von Argentinien bis Uruguay.

› **travel-library.com/south_america/**
Comprend de nombreux liens avec des guides, des galeries de photos et des cartes. Des écrivains amateurs ont par ailleurs exposé ici leurs expériences en Amérique du Sud.

› **visit-uruguay.com**
La bonne adresse pour ceux qui cherchent un hôtel dans les centres de vacances d'Uruguay. De plus, visite virtuelle dans Montevideo, horaires des bus et adresses de location de voitures.

› **wnsouthamerica.com**
Presque aussi bien que le téléscripteur d'une agence de presse. Vous pouvez obtenir ici les nouvelles de tous les pays. Liens avec des galeries de photo, des stations de radio et des agences de voyages de l'Argentine à l'Uruguay.

TASCHEN Web Picks:
Surfen Sie nach Südamerika – der faszinierende Kontinent ist nur ein paar Klicks entfernt! Die Webtipps auf diesen Seiten bringen Sie zum Beispiel in die Metropolen Argentiniens und Brasiliens, zu den Gipfeln Patagoniens und in den Dschungel Ecuadors. Wer seine Liebe zu einem dieser Ziele entdeckt hat, kann sich online auch über die jeweilige Kunst und Kultur informieren und sogar Spanisch oder Portugiesisch lernen.

TASCHEN Web Picks:
Surfez vers l'Amérique du Sud, découvrez ce continent fascinant en cliquant sur les sites web que nous vous proposons. Ils vous conduiront dans les métropoles de l'Argentine et du Brésil, sur les sommets de Patagonie et dans la jungle de l'Équateur. Quand vous aurez trouvé votre préférence pour l'une de ces destinations, vous pourrez ensuite vous informer sur l'art et la culture du pays, et même apprendre l'espagnol ou le portugais.